VOLUNTEERING
Global citizenship in action

CULTURAL RELATIONS

In the UK, we do not have a common definition of the word 'volunteering', but there is a common understanding that it involves working without financial gain and in activities that provide benefit for the wider community. Global Xchange provides young people with the opportunity to do this but also accepts the reality that the wider community is now a global community. Designed and managed in partnership with VSO, the programme aims to educate young people, through volunteering and social action, to become active *global* citizens.

At a time when global challenges such as climate change, terrorism and rising economic inequality have become commonplace in everyday news, we see that developments in the world are not automatically leading to greater benefit for all and that some problems seem more all-encompassing and more difficult to tackle than we would have admitted a few decades ago. It will take ideas, innovation and most of all commitment to making a positive contribution to tackle challenges of the scale we are now facing. This commitment needs to be a collective one and one that is based on understanding – the kind of understanding that can be developed only through a genuine dialogue.

Since the first Global Xchange in 2005, there has been a total of 35 exchanges involving 590 volunteers, 426 host homes, 376 volunteer placements and 54 communities worldwide, in 24 UK communities and 16 overseas countries. The figures themselves offer impressive testimony, but for every statistic there are wider and even more compelling stories of great human endeavour and accomplishment. The volunteers on that programme have been – and are – motivated by purposes that go well beyond any material reward, and it is to their eternal credit that they mix idealism in conviction with realism in commitment.

We need to understand that countless young people want to engage with the world: they want to play their part in bringing understanding between peoples and cultures; and they believe that international volunteering is a way of achieving change for the better. The programme demonstrates the willingness of young people to get involved in activities that effect positive change. It raises awareness of issues that don't just have an impact on them at a local level, but that affect people on the other side of the planet as well. Moving beyond the traditional approach of young people from developed countries

A Sri Lankan and UK team perform a play for the Global Xchange event in London to represent their experiences in the UK phase in Hounslow. Based loosely on *Romeo and Juliet*, Shakespeare's play, but performed in mime, it highlighted the different tensions within Hounslow and how the volunteers had tried to bring people together across these divides.

travelling to less developed parts of the world to volunteer, the programme enables young people from both sides of the wealth divide to work together in transforming their lives and the lives of others.

This is creating and nurturing genuine global partnerships and networks of young people, which are so urgently needed to tackle the problems we are facing today. Volunteers will be well-placed to carry through some of the necessary changes, because many of them will go on to occupy positions of influence and leadership. This is because of the skills and experience acquired in Global Xchange, but also because of their motives for volunteering in the first place.

We believe that it is important to help our young people become active global citizens who understand the reality of the world they live in. Who realise that while their efforts cannot eliminate all the ills of the world, they can definitely help cure some. That's the cause that all pragmatic idealists and spirited realists need to serve. We are pleased and privileged to provide a little assistance in helping young people make their contribution. It is in them that the power of a better future lies.

Martin Davidson CMG
Chief Executive, British Council

An Education Activity Day in a Sri Lankan Buddhist temple, where volunteers teach each other about a subject connected to their work. Here, volunteers are teaching their peers about Sri Lankan alternative traditional medicine – Ayurveda. © Jon Spaull/VSO

Having started as a young people's organisation, VSO has spent the last 40 years recruiting more and more experienced people, until by the late 1990s there was simply no room for people under 25 in VSO's work. We had responded to the changing needs of developing countries, at least at the obvious levels of technical and professional skills required, but had neither engaged with the British leaders, opinion-formers or citizens of tomorrow, nor with young Africans and Asians as participants rather than beneficiaries.

A new approach to engaging young people was needed – one that was relevant to the 21st century rather than the 1950s, when VSO first sent school leavers overseas. Thus, Global Xchange – a collaboration between VSO, the British Council and a number of local partners worldwide – was initiated.

I took some convincing in the early days. The programme created quite a challenge for our staff – especially our publicity people, who had to convince people that while VSO was no longer a young people's organisation, our most newsworthy programme was all about young people. And it was hard for our funders. Our biggest grant comes from the Department for International Development (DFID), and the funding agreement had only one prohibition: that the money was not to be spent on youth programming.

As we, and DFID, saw the value of engaging with young people as *participants* rather than recipients; as we saw the emergence of genuine sharing and reciprocity, that agencies are very good at talking about but less good at engendering; and as we saw the impact on the individuals and the communities they worked in – even the hardest critics began to understand that what we had was a very special programme. And we all began to talk with real pride of VSO involving volunteers from 18 to 75, rather than rushing in with disclaimers about participants not being 'proper' volunteers.

Global Xchange is now an integral and essential part of VSO's work and the partnership with the British Council has been a valuable one that has stood the test of time. It brings out the best of both agencies. It may well be that the programme is still with us in 50 years – when the rest of our work is history.

Mark Goldring
Chief Executive, VSO

CONTENTS

ACKNOWLEDGEMENTS

We are deeply grateful to Global Xchange, which was the programme that inspired our publication. We would like to especially thank Tina Murphy, Jakira Khanam, Tom Miscioscia and Jeremy Barnett, from the Global Xchange team at the British Council; Marion O'Donnell for her role in creating Global Xchange and Tom Smith and colleagues from VSO.

Our thanks go first and foremost to all the volunteers and volunteering organisations that we interviewed for this book. It would be impossible to name them all. Without their insights, this book could never have taken its current shape.

We are grateful to Ali Fisher from Mappa Mundi Consultants for the idea, and to Rachel Stevens, Mina Patria and Patrick Robinson for their initial vision, research and concept.

We would like to thank our colleagues at Counterpoint: Kate McGowan for her support throughout the project, and Gavin Moorhead for his research and contribution to the writing process. We are also grateful to those colleagues that gave support and feedback, especially Magnus Slingsby and Maja Schachner.

And finally we would like to thank all those who are working as volunteers, or with volunteers, whose voices rarely get heard. They are the true agents for change.

FOREWORD

Jon Snow

The instruction sounded pretty crazy to me. 'Turn up under the clock on the main concourse at London's Waterloo station, a few seconds before 8.30 a.m.' So we did at the very height of the commuter rush hour. There were perhaps a hundred of us and apparently we were going to participate in a spontaneous 'flashmob'. Suddenly a whistle blew and everyone surged into a bunch throwing our arms in the air, jumping as high as we could, shouting 'VSO! VSO! VSO!' The police were stunned and gasped and the commuters stopped in their tracks, others piling into them from behind, as volunteers dashed among them handing out leaflets. We must have looked as mad as hatters, but it certainly had an effect.

How many erstwhile commuters find themselves now toiling under the midday sun in Sierra Leone or somewhere outside Chennai, I don't know. This was an awareness-raising exercise. It was a loud and far cry from my own first experience of international volunteering somewhere deep in the African bush on the banks of the Nile 40 years ago.

In those days, fewer people committed themselves to a year or more of volunteering overseas. But for those who did, it was intense and generally well organised between host and volunteer countries. Now, we even see some volunteers coming to Britain from the developing world to work in inner-city projects. But the numbers of international volunteers, for example, are small, at most a couple of thousand altogether, and while there are a variety of other committed volunteer groups, there's also a mass market in what I term the generally less involved form of volunteering. These programmes all too often consist of a less than rewarding few weeks or months of vague 'helping' squeezed into a far-flung adventure trip. Most of these operations are commercial enterprises, and a good few of them, stretch the concept of volunteering extremely thinly.

But what the take-up of these trips by youngsters in the Western world tells us is that potentially there is a massive pool of young people prepared to contemplate giving their energy and capacity to assist others and learn from them at the same time.

My hope is that this will see the dawn of a new age of volunteering in which we will retrieve the high ambitions annunciated by US President John F. Kennedy when he established the Peace Corps. Surely with the worldwide web, the mobile phone and more, 'nation can speak unto nation' about precisely what is needed. I would like to see a scheme on the scale of what once was known in the UK as National Service. I want to see a worldwide scheme that enables tens of thousands of volunteers to move from North to South and from South to North. And instead of young Northern youngsters raising funds for what is essentially an indulgent 'gap' year between school and university, they would make the focus of that year a significant and intensive spell of volunteering. For volunteering brings people together in unforgettable experiences and provides its own fair share of travel, people, and places. I'd even like to see more time made available to enable a good number of youngsters to get deeply involved for 18 months or more – perhaps at the end to receive a volunteering diploma that would gain high credit on any curriculum vitae.

Some may ask, but what skills can I bring? My only answer remains, even to this day: come to my secondary school at Namasagali, where I taught so long ago on VSO. I found when I went back a couple of years ago that the need remains absolutely as great as it was then. They are hungry for information and education and still short of the resource to enable them to find it, and we have it to give from within us. From the environment programmes to irrigation, we have no idea what we can do until we make the offer. As John F. Kennedy might have said: 'Ask not what you can do for yourself; ask what you can do for someone else's life chances.'

INTRODUCTION

INTRODUCTION

You will have picked this book up and started to read it because you are interested in volunteering. Perhaps you are thinking of becoming a volunteer, or you have already had some experience of volunteering. Perhaps you work with an organisation managing a volunteering programme. Or maybe you think that somewhere in the phrase 'global citizenship' is contained the key to understanding a new way of changing the world for the better. For you we have tried to write a book we hope you will find informative, thought-provoking and useful. Before you start, just a word about what the book tries to do and what it does not, and about how to find your way around it.

We have written *Volunteering: global citizenship in action* in an attempt to demonstrate the full potential of the relationship between volunteering and active citizenship on a global stage. This has meant thinking about it in its widest sense. We have decided to conduct our own interviews, and gather our own or use existing material, because the words of those working in the field of volunteering are often the most vivid, revealing and insightful.

Among many resources that we have drawn on, one of the richest has been the archives of the international volunteering programme, Global Xchange, which is run by the British Council and VSO. It is quite unusual among volunteering programmes because reciprocity lies at the heart of Global Xchange, with UK volunteers paired with counterparts from the other participating country on each exchange, working together in volunteer placements in a selected location. The Global Xchange archive, which grows with every new exchange, has a wealth of testimonies to the power of intercultural dialogue and social action. It has become a treasury of insights into what motivates those who volunteer and why people-to-people cultural relations is such an important long-term objective.

So, one of our aims was to illuminate some of the world-changing and intercultural dimensions of volunteering that we are beginning to glimpse at the start of this century. Another was to show the latent power of intercultural dialogue when volunteers work together from different cultures in a structured environment. Much writing about volunteering concentrates either on a national perspective or on the North–South flow; from developed to the developing nations. We wanted to show, wherever we could, how much volunteers from the South could offer the increasingly diverse and fragmentary societies of 'the North'

Global Xchange volunteers working in Hounslow, England, as part of the UK–Bangladesh exchange.

in terms of new ideas and international perspectives.

The words of volunteers themselves are especially inspiring and stimulating. This is why we include them wherever we can, either in the argument of the text or in highlight boxes. Their names have generally been withheld to protect confidentiality. However, their testimonies and opinions work best in a context and so we have set them in a sequence of thinking about how volunteering is an expression of active global citizenship. The aim was to be as fresh and immediate as possible. There is a summary of the five chapters below.

Wherever a big idea or term seems to us to need some attention, rather than break up the flow, we have introduced a small number of 'concept' boxes, for example on globalisation, or cosmopolitanism. The idea was not to write an academic study of the subject or compete with some excellent recent surveys. However, we do refer to these for those wanting to follow up an interest.

In our thinking we have tried to be open and suggest possibilities rather than dictate the conclusion a reader should come to. This is especially important because, although we are writing the book in English and here in London, we wanted to address an international audience. It was important to avoid giving the impression that we have a monopoly on the interpretation of words and concepts, in particular 'volunteering' and 'active global citizenship'. To make the point, and to enrich our text with a global perspective, we invited people from different cultures to explain the word 'volunteering'. The words they used

and the comments they made can be found throughout the book.
We have also devoted a whole chapter to investigating global citizenship.

The following gives a short summary of each chapter.

Chapter 1
Act local, think global

The extreme interdependence of people in a global system is
often highlighted when ordinary life is disrupted by a natural disaster,
a major pollution incident or by disputes over the supply of natural
resources. All these events cross national borders, either in their
social, their economic or their political implications. Phenomena of
this kind, together with the opportunity to consume such a wide
array of imported products, contribute to create a distinct awareness
of globalisation. They make us especially aware of how uneven the
process of globalisation is. We note the importance of 'the Pareto
improvement', the situation when the living conditions for one are
improved without affecting or diminishing the living conditions
of another. The possibility of global citizenship, by being a tradition
of civil empowerment, with roles to play for everyone, could challenge
these inequalities. We look at various examples of how citizens become
engaged in social action, an activity that is part of being an active
global citizen. Some examples are historical, leading from Diogenes's
statement in Ancient Greece about being a citizen of the world,
to movements of civil disobedience. We then move to this century
to feature examples from Global Xchange. We then consider definitions
of volunteering from volunteers and others and suggest the idea
of a spectrum of civic engagement from relatively simple donations
to strategically planned action. Unevenness of globalisation will always
be a call for engagement in the volunteering sector as long as it is
able to make a difference.

Chapter 2
Why volunteer?

We try to answer the question of what qualities make a good volunteer
by considering the answers of volunteers themselves and those who
work with them – the former claim that no special qualities are needed
in the sense that anyone could and should volunteer; the latter claim
that the exceptional volunteer is distinguished by, among other things,
selflessness. The modesty of the former may confirm the observation
of the latter. It is also about being open and deferring judgment.
We consider morality: whether it is innately human and how universal
the ideas of good and bad are. Stereotypes are a necessary part of

human perception together with other measures the mind takes to make the world less complex in our thinking. We look at how cultural awareness can help us move beyond limiting perspectives. We look at parallels to the concept of volunteering in Africa, and the Philippines, and at the kinds of religious motivation. While personal motivations are important, they function as internal triggers to initial involvement, which are then transformed in the collective action to change the life of a community.

Chapter 3
How to get involved

Volunteering is managed by organisations of every size and kind (see also our short directory of organisations at the back of this book, derived from the implementing partners of Global Xchange and those interviewed for this book). They can be governmental, non-governmental, private enterprise, national or transnational, and be motivated by religion, politics or by philanthropy. Some are rooted in historical events or epochs; some attract the young, or the professionally skilled, or those who are retired or marginalised in society, such as prisoners who want to volunteer in the community. One of the 'drivers' of change among the international community of organisations is the leadership of the United Nation's Millennium Development Goals initiative. We profile and examine aspects of organisations in the UK (Scotland and England), South Africa, Mozambique, India, the Philippines and Brazil. We note that volunteering organisations are increasing the scope of their partnerships with a range of national and international partners and are developing their strategies to attract more volunteers by removing some of the barriers that exist and raising the quality of structured opportunities to participate. We consider the three sectors – public, private and third – and note the need for a greater collaboration (also discussed in Chapter 5).

Chapter 4
Global citizens

Globalisation brings with it the possibility of a new kind of consciousness. Cultures previously separated by space, are interacting more frequently whether face-to-face or through new communication media. We consider the claims of cosmopolitanism and suggest the need for a Global Citizenship Framework. We give an example from Global Xchange, developed in co-operation with Oxfam, which focuses on five themes: poverty and inequality; diversity; community development; volunteering; and social action. These are explained. We then turn to the way the term is used in different cultures. To some extent it depends on clarifying the meaning of the term citizenship in global contexts. The word 'global' modifies the word 'citizenship' in a new way. It suggests a metaphorical extension of the way citizenship functions within a nation state to a global situation that is still forming. We list Richard Falk's five areas of global citizenship, and we note the categories of international government organisation; international non-governmental organisation; and corporate global citizenship. We also take a look at the fair trade and the microcredit initiatives as indicative global movements.

Chapter 5
The future

We ask: what would be the best co-ordination of activity to ensure sustainability and impact in the future? Civil society is being propelled into new dimensions, and new communication technology enables the sharing of best practice and achievements around the world on a new scale. It also facilitates the co-ordination of advocacy and campaigns with potential unprecedented consequences. We consider the involvement of citizens as partners in international development and the ways in which governments are seeking to encourage participation. A new era of international co-operation could coincide with the possibility of greater integration of the three sectors: civil society, private enterprise and public services. A range of new aspirations exist, and projects are being funded that have wider social benefit built in to their delivery. Global citizenship and volunteering do have enormous impact but they are lived most intensely at the level of individual behaviour. Their success depends on individuals making the right moral choices. However, the ultimate prize to be gained happens when individuals come together to take collective action for the good of the wider global community.

Aurélie Bröckerhoff
Nick Wadham-Smith
British Council
April 2008

CHAPTER 1

ACT LOCAL, THINK GLOBAL

Global Xchange volunteers, Jennifer and Thonko, carry water. © Simon Rawles/VSO

ACT LOCAL, THINK GLOBAL

When the tsunami wave hit, it took only a short period of time for volunteers from all over the world to reach the devastated shores and help the local communities. After earthquakes, people volunteer their services to help rebuild those destroyed areas. Floodings always attract helpers from neighbouring countries, as was seen when the river Elbe in Germany overflowed and many helpers from bordering countries volunteered their services. But not only natural disasters generate an increase in voluntary services. Social issues such as HIV and Aids, malnutrition and human rights violations have also been addressed both by local communities as well as overseas voluntary organisations. Child poverty, a rising social concern in many areas of the world, and human trafficking have risen to become an important focus of European attention as a result of voluntary effort by NGOs and other non-profit organisations.

> **Volunteering**
> Helping; giving your time; giving service; missionary work
> UK

These are only a few examples of events where volunteers have helped to make a difference. For the 20th century alone, one could find hundreds of similar examples, the most spectacular being the independence movement in India, led by Mahatma Gandhi; Martin Luther King's civil rights movement in the United States in the 1960s; the end of the apartheid rule in South Africa; or, more recently, the struggle for democracy in Burma, led by activist Aung San Suu Kyi. All these have shown the impact that grass-roots movements can have on a society.

To be a volunteer nowadays is to be constantly aware of globalisation. Globalisation is one of the buzz words of our time. We get our clothes 'Made in China', or our technology 'Made in Taiwan'. We eat bananas from Latin America, watch American films and sleep on Swedish beds. Singapore imports about 50 per cent of its water from Malaysia, European imports of gas come mainly from the former Soviet Union and Japan depends entirely on imports of iron ore and coal – with Australia as the largest supplier, providing over 60 per cent of each. The rise of more efficient transport, information and communication technologies has allowed us to not only hear about events on the other side of the world, but has also given us the opportunity to actively participate in communities outside our own. In an ever-increasingly interconnected world, distances between places become smaller. This has significantly altered the way in which we relate to the world around us.

Towards a global awareness

Turning a blind eye to social injustice and unequal opportunities is virtually impossible in this global network. If, because of political struggles, Russia cuts gas exports, it will affect people outside Russia. If storms destroy a banana harvest, it will affect societies on the other side of the world. If labour exploitation is unveiled in textile production, this immediately exercises a direct influence on consumers in other countries. Therefore, volunteers strive to redefine themselves within these new parameters and renegotiate their responsibilities, not purely on a local level, but also as citizens of this transformed, accessible and 'smaller' world. As Kofi Annan once said:

> 'The challenges of our age are global; they transcend national frontiers; they are problems without passports. To address them, we need blueprints without borders. That is why, more than ever before, we need dedicated and talented young men

UK VOLUNTEERING – FACTS AND FIGURES [1]

Definitions

Informal volunteering – giving unpaid help as an individual to someone who is not a relative.

Formal volunteering – giving unpaid help through groups, clubs or organisations to benefit other people or the environment. [2]

Statistics

- Over half the population in England volunteer. In 2005, 68 per cent of people in England (or 27.4 million people) volunteered informally, while 44 per cent of people (or 17.9 million people in England) volunteered formally.

- Volunteering is popular with young and old. Fifty-three per cent of young people aged 16 to 19 have volunteered with a club or organisation at least once in the last 12 months, while 78 per cent have given unpaid help on an informal basis.

- Twenty-eight per cent of over 75s have volunteered with a club or organisation at least once in the last 12 months, while 46 per cent have given unpaid help on an informal basis.[3]

- More people are volunteering through their employer. In 2005, approximately 40 per cent of employees participated in employer-supported volunteering schemes in England. Seventeen per cent of these employees had volunteered regularly throughout the year.[4]

- Over 42,305 students volunteer through organised volunteering programmes at their university or college. Each student volunteer gives on average 81.78 hours a year to their community, contributing nearly £1,000 each a year to the economy.[5]

and women to be global citizens who make the choice of
service to humankind.'

Globalisation describes the growing interdependence of individuals,
countries and regions of the world. It is viewed as an era resulting from
rapid global developments in production, consumption, technology,
communication, transportation, employment, culture and lifestyle.

As a consequence of globalisation, actions in one locality are
having a growing impact on other distant localities. The increasing
power of global, transnational and international processes also means
that national economic and political power is being eroded. The world
is also being increasingly confronted by issues that transcend national
boundaries and which require an international response – thus, we have
international institutions such as the United Nations (UN) and the
European Union. One example is the issue of global climate change
and the 1997 Kyoto UN protocol established in response.

- Sport and recreation account for 26 per cent of all volunteering in the UK and provide
  a workforce equivalent to 180,000 full-time workers.[6]

- Volunteering is good for you. Sixty-three per cent of 25- to 34-year-olds and 62 per cent of over
  65s say volunteering helps them feel less stressed, while 71 per cent of volunteers who offer
  their professional skills and experience say volunteering helps combat depression. Nearly half
  of all volunteers say volunteering has improved their physical health and fitness.[7]

- Volunteering helps you lead a healthier life. Twenty-two per cent of 18- to 24-year-olds say
  volunteering helps them cut down on alcohol and 30 per cent say volunteering helps them
  to smoke less.[8]

- Levels of volunteering relate to levels of happiness. Research published in 2004 indicated that
  people living in areas with a high level of civic participation were happier with their lives.[9]

- One survey found that volunteering was the second greatest source of individual joy,
  behind dancing.[10]

- Six out of ten volunteers said volunteering gave them an opportunity to learn new skills.[11]

- Annually volunteering is worth over £40 billion in England and Wales. This is the equivalent
  contribution to the economy made by people involved in their local community based on the
  national average wage.[12]

- Volunteers spend an average of three working weeks a year giving unpaid help through groups,
  clubs and organisations. This is the equivalent of around one million full-time workers involved
  in their local communities.[13]

A LIST OF GLOBAL PROBLEMS

Global warming and ozone layer depletion; rapid species loss; soil erosion and desertification; pollution; population growth as a pressure on the environment and cause of poverty; world poverty, especially hunger and malnutrition and endemic diseases; HIV and Aids; racism and the associated inequalities that ensue; the status of women in many parts of the world; religious and ethnic hatred; violation of human rights, especially civil rights; economic and sexual exploitation; numerous wars; large-scale movement of refugees; international crime; international terrorism such as the events of 11 September 2001; weapons of mass destruction; proliferation of arms.

Dower, Nigel (2003) *An Introduction to Global Citizenship*, Edinburgh University Press

Throughout this process of increased interconnectedness, an acute awareness that the gains from globalisation are very unevenly distributed within as well as between societies has become more visible. Unfortunately, the benefits of globalisation do not obey, what in economic terms is called 'a Pareto improvement'. A Pareto improvement is achieved when the conditions for one human being are improved without harming those of another person. But the benefits of globalisation don't operate in such a way; they do not increase the well-being of one person, without affecting, and diminishing the well-being of another person. Globalisation is yet to become a win–win situation that does not produce winners and losers. The now somewhat famous '80–20 rule' states that 80 per cent of the global population earns only 20 per cent of global income, and within many countries there is a large gap between rich and poor.

It is apparent that there are many different definitions of globalisation and many different views about its extent as well as its costs and benefits. It is certainly the case that globalisation has been an uneven process and has benefited some more than others. It is also apparent that globalisation has not been necessarily 'global' and is often viewed as a Western phenomenon. Indeed, it is our responsibility as global citizens to play a part in spreading the potential benefits of globalisation to communities worldwide.[14]

As a result, many people have increasingly felt the need to not just address and influence issues at home, but also those that affect people on a national, and especially global level – the global citizens. 'Global citizenship' has become a term very much in vogue in recent years and its influence is rising. It has throughout history had many advocates; in a now almost legendary incident, Diogenes, the Ancient Greek philosopher, was asked where he was from. His reply was 'I am a citizen of the world', making him perhaps the first person to use the term 'cosmopolitan'.[15] To Diogenes, this meant that he felt no sense of belonging to a particular place, but rather saw his roots of identity in humanity. It was an attempt to detach human values from institutions, but did not necessarily refer to an active participation in world events outside Greece. He rather believed that society as such had corrupted human nature and that we should therefore return to natural living.

Since Diogenes's days, much has changed. Not only have most countries in the world increased our connectedness to societal institutions, these networks have also become bigger, more widespread and complex over time. Our infrastructure and exchange systems have made it much easier to be aware of events far away from where we live. Not only can we participate and shape societies that are different from our own, we can even do so without being physically present.

The increase in global networks has made global interactions easier overall. This applies to all layers of our lives, whether personal, professional, social or cultural. Ease of communication across borders has facilitated political, economic and cultural co-operation between nations. But over the last decades, speed of interaction and interconnectedness has also greatly increased the complexity of those networks, often at the cost of transparency. This loss of clarity has not only led to a resurgence in civic engagement, but also shown a need to consider the implications of being part of global systems. The need for management structures on a global level has been requested from politicians and corporations as well as civic people. These could help

> **волонтери (Volonteri)**
> Volunteering
> MACEDONIA

GLOBALISATION

Globalisation is the increasing interconnectedness of everyone and everything, brought about by increased flows of knowledge, technology, capital and integration of ideas and people around the globe. But how does this process affect each of us? At the level of our family and the people we interact with daily, we are recognising these changes. New cultures, traditions and people are filtering into our communities with increasing intensity, bringing with them different foods, clothing, languages and cultures. We are also visiting or moving into other communities around the world and taking our own experiences with us. For example, you do not have to go to Spain to eat paella – you can buy the ingredients in your local market or go to a local Spanish restaurant. Or you might find that your best friend at school is from Mauritius. Such cultural exchanges have always happened, but the difference today is that they are much easier and cheaper, and consequently, much more common and widespread. It has truly made us part of a wider network than before. This has at the same time opened our eyes to the inequalities that prevail around the globe. How do we need to address these issues in the new global order? What are our duties to the less advantaged?

re-establish clarity and assist in the exchange of information and knowledge. Providing a stronger link between societies worldwide can help make people feel more aware of their role on a global level.

The concept of global citizenship as such is rooted in a belief that everyone has their role to play in ensuring the future of our planet and the well-being of its inhabitants. The story of global citizenship is very much a story of civil empowerment. Global citizens have an awareness and understanding of the issues that have an impact not just in their own community, but also those that affect people globally. They will ensure the exchange and sharing of experiences from across the world and put the gained knowledge into action to contribute to a better future.

So, global citizens do more than just acknowledge that we are citizens of the world, they recognise where there's a need and spring to action. They realise that they cannot dissociate themselves from the wider community. According to Global Xchange, the volunteering exchange jointly run by the British Council and VSO, global citizens are 'individuals who learn from the experience of others around the world, have an awareness of issues facing developed and developing countries, and put that learning into action'.

Global citizens do not just see and understand the issues that affect the planet as a whole or parts of the world. They act upon this knowledge and try to improve the standards of living for the less advantaged. They think global and act local.

> '[Global citizenship] goes beyond simply knowing that we are citizens of the globe to an acknowledgement of our responsibilities both to each other and to the Earth itself. Global citizenship is about understanding the need to tackle injustice and inequality, and having the desire and ability to work actively to do so. It is about valuing the Earth as precious and unique, and safeguarding the future for those coming after us. Global citizenship is a way of thinking and behaving. It is an outlook on life, a belief that we can make a difference.' [16]

Here we want to make a very important point and it is an intercultural one. The concept of global citizenship flows from the actions and beliefs of volunteers. It is effective as a term only if it is owned and defined by them in terms appropriate to their cultures. To put it simply: we must not get hung up on words. For example, the phrase *global citizenship* may have a negative meaning in some societies: for example in former Soviet countries where a concept of citizenship was strictly imposed from above. It is the idea that matters, whatever it is called in

Action expresses priorities.

MAHATMA GANDHI

different cultures, and any group of volunteers will want to check their common understanding of the ideas summed up by the phrase.

How local actions have a global impact

We have seen how local actions can make a difference on a global level. For example Mahatma Gandhi and *satyagraha*, his movement of non-violent resistance, began as a small movement of local protests and manifestations. Literally translated from Sanskrit, the word *satyagraha* means to 'hold on to the truth' and the concept involves the defiance of violence as well as appealing to our rational side. Both these things begin on a personal level, for example, I refuse to beat someone no matter how much they provoke my anger, or rather than shouting at someone I try to explain my point of view. This is how Gandhi started on a very personal level himself, before gathering followers to his philosophy. He stressed the idea of civil disobedience, asking people to refuse to take part in what they believe to be corrupt systems. He did not stress, however, that we should remove ourselves from communication with the creators of such corrupt systems if we feel that we can make a difference. We should condemn wrongdoing, but not the person that has done wrong. In Gandhi's words: 'Hate the sin, love the sinner.'

Gandhi's ideas very much support the idea of civil empowerment and the belief that what we do on an individual level has larger implications for others. As part of a community, whatever we do will affect others. For example, if we believe that local farmers are suffering as a result of agricultural imports from overseas and we believe that the system from which we buy our fruit and vegetables is corrupt, then we should not buy our fruit and vegetables from these places. Instead, we could buy from an organic farm near to our home. We should question the imports of produce under doubtful circumstances and make our point of view accessible to other people around us and express our decisions towards those in charge. In this way, we may have a chance to influence the agricultural sector to make a difference.

Gandhi believed that all people should have an awareness of their everyday systems and it is everyone's duty to help shape and change these, if there is a need. Our personal attitude and awareness matter. And if many people come to a similar conclusion and express their views, we have the chance to transform what we see as unjust. [17]

History is full of people who believed in the idea that what we do as individuals can have a strong impact on the way society is run. What these people have in common is their understanding that they form part of a wider community and that they should take responsibility for their actions and consider the impact their actions have on others.

Fenner Brockway spent a lifetime campaigning against all forms of injustice not just within the UK, but also overseas. His conviction to making a positive contribution to the world led him so far as to consider himself not an individual, but a world citizen.

Aung San Suu Kyi and her desire to make a difference led her to spend much of her life imprisoned. She is inspired by Gandhi's *satyagraha* in as much that she is willing to suffer personally for what she believes to be a good cause, namely establishing democracy in Burma.

Volunteering can be a strong motor for making a difference. The Xhosa, a people indigenous to South Africa, have a proverb that reflects the idea that many people doing small things in many places can change the face of the world. In Germany, every child in kindergarten learns to sing a song based on the proverb.

The belief that volunteering projects are more than just a sum of their parts and contribute to overall betterment is at the heart of volunteering. How many times though do we hear someone question their personal potential to make a difference? 'Why should I care? I can't make a difference anyway. Unless everyone else does it, I won't be able to change anything.'

FENNER BROCKWAY

From his birth in Calcutta, India, in 1888 to his death in Hertfordshire, England, in 1988, Fenner Brockway lived during a turbulent period in human social history, a period that he helped to shape. He is widely respected both as a conscientious objector who was sentenced to jail terms during the First World War for his pacifist beliefs and as a Member of Parliament (1929–31 and 1950–64) campaigning against all forms of inequality. He was a committed humanist and a member of the British Humanist Association.

What distinguishes Fenner Brockway is his passion for humanity, and his desire to do what he can to make the world more just. He did not see himself as an individual but as a world citizen, tirelessly campaigning for world peace and equality. He once wrote of an intense personal moment when he experienced the beauty of nature: 'My philosophy is founded on the experience … I cannot be other than a world citizen, identifying with all peoples.'

Fenner Brockway spent his life campaigning for all forms of equality, including women's suffrage, an end to the apartheid rule in South Africa, against fascism in Spain, Indian independence and against imperialism. He was also a co-founder of the organisation Campaign for Nuclear Disarmament (CND), an organisation that is especially relevant today. He has left an inspirational legacy in the numerous books he wrote, inspiring future socialists, peace activists and human rights advocators.[18]

PROFILE

AUNG SAN SUU KYI

Aung San Suu Kyi is a Burmese leader for non-violent movements and an activist for democracy. She has been a prisoner of conscience in Burma for many years. In 1991, she was awarded the Nobel Peace Prize. At the end of 2007, there were rumours that Burma would be holding elections in the near future, perhaps proof of how Aung San Suu Kyi's efforts have been vindicated.

Volunteering can help us break through these thought patterns that inhibit action. Volunteering can help us realise that even one person can make a difference. It is not about necessarily achieving the big things immediately, but about making small things matter here and now. A house, after all, is built brick by brick. Although each single brick by itself may not seem like much, together they form a house.

Volunteering helps you realise that your actions contribute to something bigger – the house – and that many people around you aspire to the same goals. One of the volunteers we interviewed for this publication said:

'The most important change in myself was the realisation that little everyday choices in my life count. This includes, for example, to openly disapprove of crude jokes that are insensitive to gender, sexuality, race or religion.'

Sergio Vieira de Mello was a person who realised that our everyday choices matter. He not only lived to be a role model for other people, he was also actively concerned about promoting active involvement in peaceful coexistence and co-operation between communities, religions and cultures.

Volunteering definition

We have talked a lot about volunteering to make a difference. But what exactly do we mean by that? When looking at the contribution that volunteering can make to raise awareness of global issues and impel people to act upon what they perceive as unjust, we need to be clear about what our understanding of volunteering is.

Shesha kormi
Free-will worker
BANGLADESH

A technical definition of volunteering, the definition we most commonly received in our interviews, is 'to give time without monetary remuneration'. But if that was all there was to volunteering, then why would, for example, approximately half of all people in the UK volunteer formally or informally at least once a month? Why would the UK government invest more than £100 million in youth volunteering? [19] Surely, there must be more to volunteering than just giving time for free?

SERGIO VIEIRA DE MELLO

Sergio Vieira de Mello, or 'Sergio' as he was fondly known by his colleagues, was the United Nations High Commissioner for Human Rights (2002–03). He was a well-respected and charismatic advocate of peace and human rights as well as a highly effective humanitarian leader. He is seen to represent the principle that peace and security can be achieved through dialogue, multilateral solutions and international co-operation.

Born on 15 March 1948 in Rio de Janeiro, he joined the UN in 1969 and went on to occupy many important roles, including adviser to UN forces (Lebanon); humanitarian co-ordinator (Rwanda); special representative for Kosovo; and Head of UN Operations (East Timor). He became the United Nations High Commissioner for Human Rights in 2002, but was requested to take leave of absence from his post in 2003 to serve in Iraq as the Special Representative of the Secretary-General. He tragically died in a terrorist bomb explosion in Baghdad on 19 August 2003.

In his honour, the Sergio Vieira de Mello Prize was established in 2003, to be awarded for active involvement in peaceful coexistence and co-operation between communities, religions and cultures.

His friends and family established the Sergio Vieira de Mello Foundation to honour him and his achievements. As Kofi Annan asserts:

'Sergio dedicated his professional life to the values set out in the United Nations Charter. He never once hesitated to take on difficult, even dangerous assignments. Victims of conflict and disasters throughout the world came to know him as someone who understood their plight and knew how to deliver results despite enormous obstacles. That effectiveness was always combined with a remarkable grace and sensitivity.' [20]

Kofi Annan

When interviewing volunteers for this publication, we asked them what volunteering meant to them. We received many divergent answers to the question. Although the basic principle of giving something for free came up in almost every reply, many people from across the globe had slightly different attitudes. A young Nigerian volunteer said that to him it was 'using the resources I have for human benefit without any expectations'. This could be read as saying that volunteering is a purely altruistic activity, which only benefits the receiver. While the thought is a noble concept and an idea many volunteers subscribe to, it is doubtful that so many people across the globe would engage in purely altruistic acts, when time and monetary constraints make voluntary work much harder to fit into their lives.

Another volunteer we interviewed put it slightly differently. She defined volunteering as 'doing something for someone else without gaining anything yourself – apart from perhaps the experience of meeting new people – it is just about thinking of other people before yourself'. So while it is true that volunteering in its outset is mainly altruistic in as much that its actions are considerate of others first and foremost, every person who has previously worked as a volunteer will agree that 'the experience' of volunteering is a major gain.

What people get out of volunteering depends entirely on the individual and the situation. We can volunteer because we are passionate about a cause and are excited to actively contribute to changing it. We can volunteer because we feel grateful for what we have and want to give something back to the community. We can volunteer out of a religious sense of duty. We can volunteer just because we want to have fun, make new acquaintances and talk to people we would not necessarily meet otherwise. The list could go on.

Volunteering – it is just about thinking of other people *before* yourself.

A VOLUNTEER

The Golden Rule

Sarwar Bari, national co-ordinator of Pattan, a development organisation, defines volunteering as 'being willing to give your time or money or whatever with your free will. Volunteering is based on a concept of reciprocity.'

Every world religion has a principle of reciprocity rooted in its basic teachings. 'Putting oneself in the place of another' is a precondition of the decision-making process of a Buddhist. In Christianity, people are taught to remember that 'in everything, do to others what you would have them do to you'. In Confucianism, 'Never impose on others what you would not choose for yourself' is a basic principle, while Islamic teachings say to 'hurt no one so that no one may hurt you'. All these ask us to keep in mind other people in whatever we do.

These proverbs are collectively known as the Golden Rule, arguably the most important rule of human interaction. Although it appears to formulate a fairly basic principle, the Golden Rule has not gone

What does volunteering mean to you? Global definitions by volunteers	
'Volunteering is action for the betterment of others, for which one is not paid.' **South Africa**	'Giving time, energy and love for free. And taking responsibility when there's a need.' **England**
'My definition of volunteering consists of choice and free will of the volunteer. It means offering time and commitment in the service of a community other than the volunteer's own community. There is no financial motivation and there is regular commitment to the volunteering community.' **The Philippines**	'Volunteering is a choice people make because of interest and commitment. It is learning without a financial goal.' **Scotland**
	'It is not just about giving time and energy and money, but giving an aspect of your life that you have passion for.' **Ghana**

uncriticised throughout history. George Bernard Shaw, for example, in his 'Maxims for Revolutionists', from *Man and Superman*, denies the existence of a Golden Rule ('The golden rule is that there are no golden rules'). To him, these proverbs symbolise a fundamental lack of understanding of human nature, which is why he was eager to rephrase: 'Do not do unto others as you would expect that they should do unto you. Their tastes may not be the same.'

This strongly emphasises the need for cultural sensitivity when working with people outside our own community. We cannot expect the same rules to apply to everyone, everywhere.

No matter what our attitude towards the Golden Rule, reciprocity is one of the fundamental principles of human rights. Hans Küng drafted the 'Declaration Toward a Global Ethic' for the Parliament of the World's Religions. It is a paper that calls to mind the 1948 Universal Declaration of Human Rights and asks all people of the world to pull together for a better global order. The author states that in order to reach our full potential as human beings, we have to act with awareness, respect, sensitivity and mindfulness.

> 'For an authentically human attitude we especially call to mind that Golden Rule: What you do not wish done to yourself, do not do to others. Or positively: What you wish done to yourself, do to others! This should be the irrevocable, unconditional norm for all areas of life, for family and communities, for races, nations and religions. Self-determination and self-realisation are thoroughly legitimate – so long as they are not separated from human self-responsibility and global responsibility, from responsibility for fellow humans and nature.'[21]

For a long time, volunteering has been seen as a one-way process. Giving Christmas baskets, donations of food, money or clothing are all part of this tradition. Charity was regarded as a purely altruistic act for the temporary betterment of others. The focus was on how to benefit the receiver. But there seems to have been a shift in perception and practice, a move from one-off to regular engagement, from 'merely' helping others to helping others help themselves. But increasingly attention has been brought to the benefits of the volunteer as well. Now, it is often seen that volunteering can strongly benefit the volunteer and a new dictum has emerged, enabling volunteers to help themselves before they can then help others to help themselves.

In the essay 'Volunteerism, Empowerment, and Human Dignity', Robert Leigh looks at the shifts that have taken place in the perception of volunteering. Old associations are breaking up and being replaced

Volunteering is based on a concept of reciprocity.

SARWAR BARI, PAKISTAN

CULTURAL SENSITIVITY

Volunteers need intercultural skills. These are often developed during a placement, but learning to interact effectively across and between cultures is a lifelong process. It benefits both the individual and society on a long-term basis. In today's multicultural communities, these skills are essential for volunteers whether in their own or another country. At the heart of success lie two questions: what makes us different and what makes us the same as each other, as human beings?

Difference is not always just about culture – we can be aware of differences of gender and disability, for example, especially in volunteering placements. However, becoming more culturally aware, which is what we are considering here, probably depends as much on attitude as it does on knowledge. It is always useful to know about behaviour, which can have another meaning in a different culture: visitors to Thailand should not show the soles of their feet to others; looking someone straight in the eye can signal a lack of respect in one culture and honest directness in another. Researching the history and customs of another country or culture before an encounter is always a good idea but knowledge will get you only so far and can lead to stereotyping, for example English people are cold and difficult to get to know. These signposts within cultures are useful on arrival. Volunteers who write about their experiences often express surprise at how individuals they meet or live with don't fit the rules. It is no use knowing what *shame* and *losing face* mean in a situation unless you can work through the implications in actual communication. That is where the determination to explore comes in.

There is a belief that being culturally sensitive is basically about self-censorship and avoiding risk. Quite the opposite is true: it is about being yourself and about taking risks to find out how your behaviour is interpreted by others. Those who navigate cultures best give out messages that show they are open to correction or challenge and can change their behaviour if necessary. When a group has been together for a while and trust has grown, it is possible to review the situations that caused offence or puzzlement, once emotions have cooled down. You can start a discussion about cultural differences and then discuss the problem more objectively. As in other areas of life, we learn most from mistakes and the area of intercultural understanding is no exception. Often this new awareness moves you and the group on to the next stage of understanding.

We visited a group of volunteers in Luton, near London, who are part of Global Xchange. Half the team of 18 came from Mongolia; half from all over the UK. Watching them interact at their project meetings, having worked together in both countries for nearly six months, we noticed the complex series of cues they used to translate for each other when some struggled with English. The Mongolians had been the translators for the British group in Mongolia and strong cross-cultural skills had developed. This UK–Mongolian group was also noticeably more tactile than just a UK group would have been, suggesting they had negotiated, quite literally, how close they wanted to be to each other.

Educationists have considered how intercultural skills might be developed. They put an emphasis on skills of interpreting situations; knowing how to find things out; making critical comparisons; and the skill of developing self-awareness. Many placements in different cultures can go badly wrong. It is possibly this last skill – getting to know yourself, your own culture and values – which provides the best inoculation against culture shock and contributes most to intercultural understanding.

by new ideas of what the benefits of volunteering can be to both sides. He sees a 'gradual shift towards an expression of volunteering as a two-way process, with benefits generally accruing to the person doing the volunteering, as well as to the person on whose behalf the volunteer act is being taken'. He understands that volunteering can be a chance for the volunteer to better his or her own life by gaining skills and experience, making new friends and increasing his or her chances of employment. He further points to the fact that volunteering can be an agent for social cohesion as it can give people that are excluded from mainstream society a means of participating in areas they would normally not be a part of.

> 'For many people voluntary action is a means of making friends, gaining skills, experience and confidence, increasing chances of employment, enhancing one's standing in the community, or even living longer. But for many other people, excluded from mainstream society for reasons of income, education health, age, gender, or race, to volunteer can also be a tremendously empowering experience and a means of acquiring the most basic notions of dignity.' [22]

What this tells us is something important. When people feel that they are making a valuable contribution, they are not only more likely to be motivated and keep volunteering, but also find that it gives meaning to their own lives and raises levels of happiness and well-being. Many different volunteering organisations have incorporated this idea in their programmes. The belief that volunteering can bring about social cohesion can be seen from programmes that are run for serving prisoners, the elderly, young children or people from a deprived socio-economic background.

The volunteering we are looking at in this book is part of this circle of reciprocity, but is more particularly looking at increasing global awareness. Although there are many different forms of volunteering, especially, in recent times, the filling of skills gaps, we want to look at how volunteering, social activism and global citizenship interact. How does volunteering affect the global order? How do concepts such as global citizenship transform the nature of volunteerism?

A spectrum of civic engagement
Volunteering can be regarded as part of a spectrum of civic engagement. At one end of the spectrum, there is charity and one-off donations – donating money after a natural disaster has devastated a region and giving clothing, blankets and food to war-torn areas.

Jaki work
Donkey work
NIGERIA

Volunteers preparing
Pakistani dishes for the
community farewell.

Charity as a philanthropic act has been the norm of helping other
people throughout history. Donations of money and goods have been
practised by corporations as well as churches and individuals for
a long time. These are actions that help out people when they most
need it. They are a way of temporarily improving a situation.

But the donations are converted into items that will be consumed:
for example, clothes will wear out, food will be eaten and money will
be spent on things necessary for urgent temporary relief. And then the
pre-donation situation will be restored. Charitable giving can be like a
plaster we put over a wound – it covers up the symptoms, but doesn't
help eliminate the cause of injury. Charitable donations raise the
question of sustainability. Can one-off actions and provisions of
resources really improve someone else's life? Is that enough to help
make the world a better place? Don't we need initiatives that are aimed
at the long term? Initiatives that help people to help themselves.
Or to put it in the words of Her Majesty Queen Rania Al-Abdullah of
Jordan, who moderated a session on global citizenship during the
May 2007 World Economic Forum at the Dead Sea in Jordan: 'Does this
helping hand come in the form of a handout, that is charity, or does it
come in the form of a hand to help them along, to help them up, that is
civic engagement?'

In the middle of the spectrum are activities that provide assistance
for the long term, but don't necessarily feature as part of a structured
and strategic framework. Although these can have a lasting effect for
the person receiving the helping hand, and even the person who has

**Give a man a fish and
you feed him for a day.
Teach a man to fish
and you feed him for
a lifetime.**

CHINESE PROVERB

offered it, the activities fail to have a major impact as they do not try to tackle problems at the root. If, for example, a charity raises money on a regular basis to give to a local hospital in a rural area, then this will help improve the facilities of that hospital. If another organisation sends doctors and nurses to that school, they will help improve health and hygiene standards in the region. Both monetary donations and human capital will make a difference to that particular hospital. If both organisations decide to withdraw their aid though, the hospital will go back to where it was before, because it was dependent on the hand-out. If organisations don't ensure they provide capacity-building and development training, their actions will always be limited in time, scale and impact. To ensure longevity of betterment, yet more is needed.

The other end of the spectrum is made up from strategic approaches to civic engagement and philanthropy with a large-scale design. They are aimed at providing long-term engagement – identifying and then tackling causes of social injustice. Rather than simply covering a wound, they aspire to eliminate the cause of injury.

These strategic programmes have won increased popularity over the last few years. Those involved in the field have come to realise that occasional giving and helping must be supplemented by a more sustainable strategy. There is an equally urgent need for programmes that help to improve the way societies run and that maximise the benefit of resources for all the people and not just a selected few. For example, rather than building a local hospital and staffing it with doctors and nurses through a non-governmental organisation, a more viable alternative might be to let local people participate in planning, constructing and running the institution and train them to be doctors and nurses themselves.

Sharing our skills and expertise with others is vital to ensure that they are not dependent on us, but rather slowly learn to improve their own situations at a pace that is suitable to their cultural environment. If you make people a part of something, they will probably be more

Harambee
Self-help; pulling together; collective activity; merry-go-round/revolving fund
KENYA

WWOOF

Working Weekends on Organic Farms (WWOOF) began in the UK in 1971 when a secretary living in London wanted to spend some time in the countryside. People in New Zealand started something similar in 1973 but it was called Willing Workers on Organic Farms and it catered more for the needs of travellers and students of organic farming. This may have been because New Zealand was a more rural-based society and if New Zealanders wanted to stay on a farm there was usually a relative somewhere who offered the opportunity. From 1971 WWOOF has grown to include WWOOF exchanges in over 70 countries around the world. The WWOOF network provides a contact point for volunteers (WWOOFers) who want to live on organic farms and learn about them and other ecological and sustainable projects, and the hosts, who wish to open up their homes and welcome the WWOOFers into their daily lives, and give them hands-on experience.

WWOOF aims to:

- give people the opportunity to learn organic growing techniques at first hand
- provide everyone with the opportunity to experience living on a farm
- improve communication within the organic movement
- help individuals develop the confidence to become self-sufficient
- bring together people from all walks of life, forming new friendships and making useful contacts.

Many WWOOFing opportunities exist, from large working farms to lifestyle or homesteading properties where people are trying to be as self-sufficient as possible. In addition, WWOOF New Zealand offers a variety of organic hosts from willow weavers, eco-builders, permaculture enthusiasts and renewable energy users to an organic bakery, vineyards, breweries, craft makers and Rudolf Steiner homes.

There are WWOOFing opportunities across the world involving hosts and WWOOFers from a wide range of countries and cultures. The opportunity to meet people and learn about different cultures is an important part of a WWOOF exchange. The desire for more sustainable ways of living and the wish of travellers to experience the real culture of a country, not just to watch passively as a tourist, has contributed to the popularity of WWOOF. Comments from 'Everyone should go WWOOFing because then we would all learn how to tread lightly and look after this earth' to 'I have learned that we are all part of this global village; by immersing myself in another culture I realised that we all have the same wants and needs no matter where we are from. We all want to provide for our families, be happy, accepted, to love and to be loved' have been made about WWOOF.

Volunteering as a WWOOFer is a great way to become immersed in the daily life of others and can help people gain a better understanding of the country or region they are volunteering in, not to mention the discoveries people have made about themselves by learning about other ways of life, and other beliefs. Because WWOOFing brings together such a diverse range of people, and requires trust and respect from everyone involved, it actively promotes cultural awareness and understanding. Many WWOOFers and hosts have said that they have become more tolerant of others by being part of the WWOOF experience. This understanding and tolerance, it is hoped, leads to a more accepting and peaceful world.

WWOOFers give their time and energy to help on a farm, and the host provides meals and accommodation and shares knowledge about organics. This also contributes to the success of the WWOOF philosophy – no money changes hands. Consequently the normal roles and expectations that come with the service provider idea can work successfully.

Worldwide there are between 25,000 to 30,000 WWOOF volunteers joining every year and around 5,000 WWOOF hosts.

Here is the testimony of Yoko Suzuki, a Japanese WWOOFer who stayed at Wynova Organic Farm, New Zealand:

'My experience with WWOOF started by chance. I didn't know about WWOOF at all; I didn't even know anything about organic food. Then I met a lady at an organic shop; she was with another Japanese girl who was staying at her farm as a WWOOFer. She invited me for lunch. I visited her farm, which was the first time I had visited a farm in New Zealand. I was amazed by the huge space, open sky, and the amount and variety of vegetables and fruit trees. For the salad, she just picked greens from her garden. That salad was so delicious, made entirely with home-grown, fresh ingredients and I thought what a wonderful life – I like it.

After that I met her several times and walked through her farm, and increasingly started to be interested in farming and life at an organic farm.

I still didn't understand what WWOOF really was. I just wanted to stay there and experience everything on the farm. I had never worked at any farm; I didn't know anything about farming. Sometimes I wondered if I actually helped her at all, so I sometimes felt uncomfortable about staying there and being fed delicious food. But I enjoyed staying on the farm very much. Working on the farm made me fit and healthy (with her good food). I was satisfied every single day. Weeding huge, huge places, planting lots of trees, harvesting fruits from trees, climbing and hugging trees and so on – every experience was totally different from office work in Japan.

For me, WWOOF was a great experience, which I had never had before. It changed my life. I was never interested in living in the countryside before that, but now I live in New Zealand. I enjoy country living, vegetable gardens and living with nature. I am sure that without the experience of WWOOF, I would not be living here. I like myself and my life now. I never thought I'd feel like this.

The WWOOF programme gives you a great opportunity. You need to work, and it's not for money. You can work with your pure soul. You can taste the joy of working, which is not easy to do with normal work. You can genuinely enjoy working.'

WWOOF
Andrew and Jane
PO Box 1172
Nelson 7040
New Zealand

Telephone/fax +64 (0)3 5449890
E-mail: support@wwoof.org
www.wwoof.co.nz

passionate about it, because they feel ownership over it. And passion is one of the strongest supporters of commitment. This shows the importance of 'acting local'.

The capacity-building and development end of the spectrum requires us to 'think global'. This needs co-ordination on a more strategic level, which then provides the framework for local action to take place. Only if we know what is needed in other parts of the world, can we help make a successful contribution.

As we have mentioned before, the problems of today are crossing national borders. The integration of national economies into wider transnational systems, the increase of interconnectedness between all parts of the world – politically, socially and culturally – and increased mobility of people, all ask for a system of global governance. The rise of modern information and communication technologies, as well as an improved and increasingly dense transport system, has inextricably linked us to people from across the world.

It seems that still too few people are the winners of globalisation; a majority still lack the benefits such global structures can bring about. As part of the world community, it is our duty to step up and make a difference. Malnutrition, climate change and poverty are only a few of the problems that affect us globally. Globalisation has so far failed to deliver relief and improvement for all people of the planet. On the contrary, it has resulted in a further widening of the socio-economic gap.

At the same time, globalisation has opened up new channels of communication and interaction. We can make use of these systems – we can exchange information via media and technology, and we can share experience and skills. We can travel to impoverished places and offer a helping hand. We can help rebuild areas after natural catastrophes. We can use increasingly integrated political and economic systems to improve living standards for all people, not just a few, and spread the potential benefits of globalisation much more evenly. We can be empowered and active global citizens. We can think global, and act local.

In this chapter we have taken an overview in order to set volunteering in the context of its time. This has meant sweeping back through history to the present and also trying to grasp the complex phenomenon of globalisation. In the next chapter we come down to earth, as it were, to look more closely at human motivation, and ask why people volunteer.

Endnotes

[1] Volunteers' Week: www.volunteersweek.org.uk/About+the+Week/volunteering-facts-and-figures-.htm

[2] *Citizenship Survey*, Department for Communities and Local Government, 2005

[3] *Citizenship Survey*, Department for Communities and Local Government, 2005

[4] *Citizenship Survey*, Department for Communities and Local Government, 2005

[5] *Student Volunteering: The National Survey*, Student Volunteering England, 2003

[6] London Olympics Bid document, *Volunteering and health, happiness and skills,* 2005

[7] ICM Research findings commissioned for Community Service Volunteers and Barclays, 2004

[8] ICM Research findings commissioned for Community Service Volunteers and Barclays, 2004

[9] Economic and Social Research Council's Democracy and Participation Research Programme, 2004

[10] Argylle, M. (1996) *The Social Psychology of Leisure*, New York: Penguin Books

[11] Davis Smith, J. (1998) *The 1997 National Survey of Volunteering: Volunteering and the economy*, Institute for Volunteering Research

[12] *Home Office Citizenship Survey*, 2003

[13] *Home Office Citizenship Survey*, 2003
www.timebank.org.uk/mediacentre/research.php
www.ivr.org.uk
http://news.bbc.co.uk/1/hi/uk/909591.stm

[14] Further reading: Giddens, A. (1990) *The Consequences of Modernity*, Cambridge: Polity Press; Giddens, A. (1991) *Modernity and Self-Identity: Self and Society in the Late Modern Age*, Cambridge: Polity Press; Held, D., McGrew, A., Goldblatt, D. & Perraton, J. (1999) *Global Transformations: Politics, Economics and Culture*, Cambridge: Polity Press; Hutton, W. (2002) *The World We're In*, London: Little Brown

[15] http://san.beck.org/EC22-Aristotle.html

[16] www.oxfam.org.uk/education/gc/what_and_why/what

[17] Further reading: Kripalani, Khrishna (ed.) (2005), *Gandhi: All men are brothers,* Continuum: New York

[18] A collection of Fenner Brockway's personal papers is held at the Churchill Archives Centre – see www.chu.cam.ac.uk/archives; contact Churchill to view the papers by appointment
http://janus.lib.cam.ac.uk/db/node.xsp?id=EAD%2FGBR%2F0014%2FFEBR
www.humanism.org.uk/site/cms/contentviewarticle.asp?article=2044
www.ppu.org.uk/learn/infodocs/people/pp-fenner.html#opposingconscription2

[19] Department for Communities and Local Government, *Citizenship Survey: active communities topic report*, 2005

[20] www.sergiovdmfoundation.org/en/home.html

[21] Küng, Hans 'Declaration Toward a Global Ethic': www.weltethos.org/dat-english/03-declaration.htm

[22] www.worldvolunteerweb.org/browse/sectors/human-rights/doc/volunteerism-empowerment-and-human.html

CHAPTER 2

WHY VOLUNTEER?

'Be the change you want
to see in the world.'

MAHATMA GANDHI, 1869–1948

Global Xchange volunteers, Max and Dan, in Malawi. © Simon Rawles/VSO

WHY VOLUNTEER?

Profile of a volunteer

The statements below, which are from people who are actively involved in volunteering, are powerful pointers to what motivates them. So what is a volunteer?

We could begin by saying it is someone who gives their time, energy, resources and passion to make a contribution to global betterment as part of a reciprocal process. Volunteers recognise areas where there's a need and act upon this recognition. They do not expect to receive anything in return, especially not monetary compensation, but will usually feel that they have changed as a result of their activity.

Anyenba
Community coming together
PHILIPPINES

WHY VOLUNTEER?	
'I would like to take part in affirmative action work, addressing a key issue in my country.'	'I would like to learn to communicate in the local languages, become involved with the local community and try to make a difference.'
'I would like to travel and learn about new cultures.'	'To improve all-round personal skills, better my lifestyle, make a difference, however little, experience a new culture.'
'I want to gain professional and personal development – an experience in professional volunteering.'	
	'I really want to live by the idea of being heroes for each other. Imagine the possibility, if volunteerism was a culture?'
'To gain international exposure and awareness in the field of peace and development.'	
'I would like to become aware of the current and real situation in the community to give myself a chance to make a difference.'	'I realised that there is a need to be proactive in the community and society and that I need to have a high level of awareness about everything around me. I also feel the need to increase my level of flexibility and adaptability.'
'To make a practical contribution, to develop and share my skills, to become more confident, to adapt to living in a different culture, to learn a local language, to make the most out of the whole experience, to work hard and give my all to the project.'	
	'By doing little things and starting it right, we can create an impact in slowly changing the lives of people for the better.'
'To reflect on myself as an individual, to appreciate the things I have, to understand myself and my place in the culture.'	'To become more confident, independent and responsible, to challenge myself and explore myself and other people, to make a difference.'

They will, however, get something out of their engagement, such as contentment, new skills, friendships and enjoyment, but these things are secondary to the desire to improve overall well-being for all people and the planet.

But why do some people see the necessity of engagement with the world around us, while others don't? Why do an increasing number of people feel the need to become involved in issues related to global justice? And what distinguishes people who volunteer from those who don't?

Sandorng
Own initiative
MONGOLIA

People from all walks of life, all backgrounds and ages, all nationalities, religions and ethnicities volunteer. There is not a single segment of society that does not engage in voluntary actions of some sort. This can be a mother baking a cake for her daughter's school fair, a friend driving another friend to the other side of town, or a grandmother knitting sweaters for the local church. These and similar voluntary activities are more or less ingrained in societies across the globe. While it is certainly a good deed, what they all have in common is that the basis for engagement is a relationship between the giver and the receiver. As an interviewee pointed out to us, volunteering, in the way outlined previously, removes these personal relationships from the activity. When we talk of volunteering, we often refer to those things we do to make someone's life better without actually knowing them on a personal basis.

We are convinced that in order to fully understand the notion of volunteering, recognise the benefits of such activities and the changes that they trigger, both on a structural, but also on an individual level, it is best to give a voice to people who are volunteers themselves. They are best placed to talk about their experiences and give volunteering the realistic account it deserves.

In the interviews we conducted for this publication, we tried to examine the reasons why people volunteer, as well as compile a list of qualities that volunteers thought made a good volunteer. In both instances we received a multiplicity of answers.

What does it take?
Often, volunteers are regarded by others as having outstanding characters and personalities. They volunteer because they have traits most people lack. Whether out of admiration or as a justification for not being involved themselves, volunteers are regarded by many as special. Which is why it was interesting to hear what volunteers themselves had to say. And not necessarily surprisingly, none of the answers suggested that a good volunteer had to have an extraordinary or outstanding personality. Thabo Putu, a South African lecturer in development studies

at Witwatersrand University, said that no qualities whatsoever were required in order to volunteer – 'anyone can volunteer'. A young Egyptian volunteer was of a similar opinion: 'Everyone can get involved in volunteering at some level. It is better not to say that volunteers should have such and such a quality. Being open to a new way of thinking and a new way of leading your life and a willingness to change and have your thoughts challenged make a good volunteer.' Sue Gwaspari, UK Assistant Director, Business Development for Community Service Volunteers (CSV), one of the leading volunteering organisations in the UK, told us that it is the 'human qualities that matter. Understanding, patience and a willingness to get stuck in are what make a volunteer.'

These people have an open view of volunteering as something anyone can get involved in; they simply list a few traits that may make volunteering an easier experience. But this is not to say that anyone should just do anything. Enlarging on the qualities needed in volunteering, the lecturer at Witwatersrand University emphasised the importance of finding the right match between volunteering opportunity and potential volunteer. So he realised that good volunteering was not necessarily what happened on an individual level, but more in the way an organisation can offer a structure that gives these individual actions more impact and sustainability. This distinction between the individual and the structural levels is often made when examining the concept of volunteering. Which structures have a positive impact on volunteering; which structures inhibit the process; and what happens to us personally, as we volunteer? To understand fully the implications for both the individual and for the organisation, it is important to look at interconnections between the two levels.

A micro- and a macro-level

Taking the above statements as a basis, we can see the interplay of those two layers, micro- and macro-level. Although at first glance the statements appear fairly general, a closer look shows that they still highlight a strong relationship between the individual and the wider community they are a part of. The statement 'human qualities that matter. Understanding, patience and a willingness to get stuck in are what make a volunteer' points out the 'human qualities' that are important. This implies certain values and morals prevalent in the speaker's culture. Someone from Papua New Guinea may have a completely different list of 'human' qualities from a person in the UK.

> *Nwoa buoa*
> Help your neighbour
> GHANA

Universal human values?

Are there any human qualities that transcend boundaries and can be considered universal? The question of what makes a good human is as old as philosophical thought.

It would be false to assume that all character traits can be regarded from the same point of view in different societies and at different times. Everyone who has travelled to a country that has a culture quite alien to their own will have experienced a situation where their own ideas of politeness were met with puzzlement, shock or even suspicion. This is because our values are always part of our own cultural frames of reference.

Yet, throughout history and especially in the rise of a more interconnected world, people have always been in search for human universals. Documents such as the *Declaration Toward a Global Ethic* or the *Universal Declaration of Human Rights* are expressions of this effort to identify aspects linking all humanity.

Some thinkers (most famously Immanuel Kant, 1724–1804), state that some activities are 'right' and some 'wrong' in every context and for all of humanity. Motivations and actions rather than their outcomes are the point – the consequences do not matter so much if we perform the right action.[23] So, for example, if we were lying to someone, according to these theories, this would be morally wrong, no matter whether the person we lied to ever found out or we lied to protect that person.

The human qualities referred to previously can be seen from such a universal perspective; human qualities that may be valid throughout the world and not just framed by our own cultural references.

We asked volunteers whether they saw any such qualities within the volunteering world. Two were quoted by most volunteers: humility and respect. They were the most frequently listed qualities 'expected' from a volunteer. By being humble and respectful, we acknowledge the world around us in a non-judgemental way and allow for divergent views. Both keep us from jumping to conclusions or imposing our own views on other people. Arguably, a good volunteer is anyone who is willing to listen to what others have to say and acts with respect towards other ideas. Rather than feeling the need to be experts in a field in order to be able to make a difference, sometimes it is good to be aware of our own shortcomings and to be humble. Rather than feeling the need to show others how to do things, sometimes it is good to recognise the potential of other people, to be respectful.

Sotho/Tswana-letsema
Working together
SOUTH AFRICA

Generalising without judgement
Being unprejudiced was another quality that all interviewees mentioned when they talked about volunteering, especially overseas. Prejudice and stereotype always play a significant role when interacting with others, even more so when it happens across cultures. Most people would

agree with the statement that we should be non-judgemental and free of prejudice and stereotype in our social interaction. But is that really possible?

As we have mentioned before, we are not just individuals in a vacuum, but we are connected to wider sociocultural frameworks that shape our ideas and convictions. Thus, as social beings, we are shaped by our environment. Our norms and values are inextricably connected to those of others in our community. They are not naturally given, but created in a two-way process of negotiation and authorisation. As part of this process, we develop ideas and generalisations.

It would be asking too much of our brain to process all the details we are receiving every time we are receiving them, which is why we have structures in our brains that categorise and classify the input they receive. For example, when we see a car, our brain puts together all the

Our thoughts are unseen hands shaping the people we meet. Whatever we truly think them to be, that's what they'll become for us.

RICHARD COWPER, ENGLISH WRITER (AKA JOHN MIDDLETON MURRAY JR)

CHANGE STORIES

How people can change after volunteering and the benefits of volunteering are best described by those people who have undergone changes after a volunteering experience. We have assembled change stories from volunteers that have participated in Global Xchange. These testimonies come from people across the globe.

'Before my volunteer placement, I was somewhat conservative about English people, their culture and attitude towards third world countries, particularly Pakistan. I experienced some misinformation about Pakistan and Islamic religion, because the people getting that information from media were not necessarily projecting the true picture of Islam and Pakistan. The experience has changed my understanding of the English. English people were very open, friendly and hospitable. I never anticipated that my host mother would be so kind and caring – she was treating me like a member of her family. I couldn't express my heartfelt gratitude towards the parents of my counterpart, where I spent my Christmas days. In this respect I have become more liberal and I would say this significant change happened in my life only because of my experience as a volunteer.'

'Through volunteering placements, I was fortunate to learn about new and diverse issues, which I had no interest in prior to the programme or did not know much about, ranging from disabilities, climate change and the environment. They have taught me open-mindedness and to be a responsible global citizen with an interest in issues happening around me and globally. It has changed my mentality from that of nonchalance in political and civic matters to enthusiasm in every way. I am more than happy to say that the leadership in me has manifested itself together with new skills as a result of the experience. Ultimately, I have come to appreciate myself, my country, people and life in general.'

'The past five months as a volunteer have been a roller coaster of adventures and challenges. One of the reasons I applied to the programme was to experience a new culture different from my own and to give myself a new challenge. Working as a volunteer helped me learn about some of the issues faced by the people of Mindanao, such as mining and its benefits and dangers, the problems faced by indigenous people who want to make ancestral land claims, and much more. I have had a whale of a time and ridden my roller coaster through the ups and downs, the spins and turns.'

'It was never in my consciousness, how important volunteering is. I was even afraid to tell my parents and friends that I would be giving up six months of my life to volunteer. I did not trust NGOs much because of the thought that they are just giving their "help" as a complete front for money-making. But now, I realised that it's more than just money; it's giving high-quality time to other people, which might have a strong impact on them and eventually on the volunteers. I believe that the volunteers did not "sacrifice" even a single second of their life. It is a passion. A passion being fed by a lifetime of memories and impressions of different people from various walks of life.'

'Seeing a child smile, trying to understand and communicate with people of different beliefs, being part of a peace campaign, being able to help, having the opportunity to make changes – these are just some of the things I have learned while immersing myself in volunteering. The experience not only helped me change my perception about volunteering, but it also taught me that envisaging and acting on change will never be impossible.'

'Volunteering has changed my perception of the world. Before, I tried to highlight the cultural differences of people. But I realised actually that people even from the other side of the world have so many things in common. Now, I know that people have conflicts not because of cultural differences, but rather due to individual differences.'

'The challenges of living in a different country, eating different food, learning a new language and trying to understand a new culture in a team of ethnically, religiously and culturally diverse members, and learning more about myself and my strengths and weaknesses has created my change story. Being away from my comfort zone, made me realise a lot of things. It led me to discover little things . . . indeed my experience entails lots of events, which have made me a changed man, a better man.'

information and tells us it is a car. Rather than looking at all the details, it bundles and generalises them to let us know that we are seeing a car. In this way, these cognitive structures help us manage the vast amount of information that would otherwise have made its way to our consciousness: four wheels, made of steel, one can sit in it, it can drive at different speeds, it is red, it has windows, doors, handles on the doors, etc. If we were to process all of this every time we saw a car, our brain would soon shut down because of cognitive overload.

Therefore, generalisations can be useful. Stereotypes are a special form of generalisation that has often been connected to representing exaggerated views of particular characteristics: all Germans are disciplined, the French are romantic, Italians passionate, the Scots mean, the Irish lucky . . .

We think and make sense of others we don't know through stereotyping. And this is quite a natural process – developing generalised ideas about people that are not part of our own community. We fill in gaps of knowledge with stereotyped views. [24]

Stereotypes become a problem when we are unable to see beyond them; when they become prejudices that affect our behaviour towards others. When they are accepted as truth. History is full of examples of what can go wrong when prejudice takes over our thinking – slavery, Nazism, apartheid, to name just a few.

As mentioned before, we are social beings and our values are created through negotiation and legitimisation with others. Therefore they are not fixed and we can influence not only our own perception, but also that of others around us. The ability to rise above one's own formulaic ideas is vital if prejudice is to be overcome.

Volunteering can help with this process because, as a volunteer, we are likely to encounter people and cultures that differ significantly from our own and about which we may have stereotyped opinions. Reciprocal volunteering programmes especially have the benefit to fight stereotyping, as we work and live both in our own community, as well as overseas. This helps us to understand not only other cultures, but also allows us to look at our own opinions from an outsider's perspective. This way, we can challenge our own views as well as those of others and be open to new ideas and influences. It is acceptable not to know certain things, as long as we are willing to learn.

Change through action

We looked at some qualities that volunteers should, or rather could, have. We have established that people don't need to be extraordinarily gifted or particularly talented in any area of life. It is more the fact of actually doing something that distinguishes volunteers from other members of their community.

Often, it is the volunteering experience as such, that has made people see a change in themselves, in their perceptions and interactions with others. Often, this change has made volunteers realise their own potential and capabilities and enabled them to not only reconsider things on a personal level, but also more importantly carry this into wider parts of their community.

We are each burdened with prejudice – against the poor or the rich, the smart or the slow, the gaunt or the obese. It is natural to develop prejudices. It is noble to rise above them.

AUTHOR UNKNOWN

Why volunteer? revisited

There are almost innumerable reasons for volunteering. Personal and structural elements both play their part in why people volunteer and what kind of volunteering activity they are most likely to engage in.

Personal traits, such as the willingness to take action, are important in volunteerism, but it would be reductive to say that it is just our personality that leads us to want to make a difference by volunteering. Societal structures that lie outside the individual or current affairs can equally motivate people to take action.

In our interviews about why people were motivated to volunteer, we received a variety of answers incorporating personal, social, aspirational and cultural incentives. All these form a strong interplay and shape our work as volunteers.

Volunteering can also be an immediate reaction to what happens in our direct environment. You may just be particularly upset about a plan by local authorities to, for example, shut a library, which is why you volunteer your time to work there in order for it to remain open. Similarly, you may be particularly touched by seeing homeless people in your streets, which is why you decide to work in the local soup kitchen. On a similar note, you may spend an afternoon working in

'I grew up in Zimbabwe's second largest city, Bulawayo. We were taught at school and at home that our behaviour must be guided by the principles of humanity referred to as *hunhu* and *ubuntu* – those values that separate human beings from animals, birds and reptiles. The principle of *ubuntu* is encapsulated in phrases such as *umuntu ngumuntu ngabanye* (a person is a person through others) or proverbs such as *izandla ziyagezana* (the left hand washes the right hand and the opposite is true), all stressing the importance of communal responsibilities. *Ubuntu-hunhu* is the art of being human and belonging to life's networks, where behaviour produces ripple effects on other forms of communal existence.

It is in times of stress such as that presented by Aids in Zimbabwe that *ubuntu-hunhu* can be a resource for designing interventions. In the UK, when some policy-makers assumed that Africans would easily accept the language of Western notions of research ethics and rights, we used principles of *ubuntu-hunhu* to set a research agenda that was filtered through our ways of seeing, knowing and interpreting the world, grounded in this art of being human.'

Martha Chinouya: excerpt taken from: 'Ubuntu and the helping hands for Aids', *Under the Tree of Talking: Leadership for Change in Africa*, Counterpoint, 2007, pp. 101–111

Dr Martha Chinouya is a social scientist with vast experience in the research of human rights discourse and ethics informed by African epistemologies.

'For me, *ubuntu* is where the spirit of volunteerism comes from. You are saying: "I am not going to leave you to go without food, when I can." The *ubuntu* says: "When I have a piece of bread I would rather have half of it and you have the other half." There is the example of funerals: "I am not going to wait for someone to tell me that there is a funeral next door, that someone has passed away. I will go out there and help to comfort them. Not only comfort them, I will help draw water so that they can cook. I will go and get food. I will go and dig the grave, without expecting them to pay me." Nobody has to come and say: "Can you come help us dig the grave?" Men in the communities know – and this is still happening today – that there is a funeral and they need to go and dig the grave. Let us bring water. Let us help. Let us go and slaughter a cow. For us, that is *ubuntu* and volunteerism at its best.

If you meet a woman stuck in the middle of traffic, trying to push her car, you know that she cannot push her car. You stop your car somewhere and help. You do not ask to be paid. She never invited you to do it, but you do it because you want to do it. That is what *ubuntu* is about. When I look at *ubuntu* and I look at volunteerism, I see one thing.'

Thabo Putu, South Africa

a local park to keep it clean and beautiful. These may seem like small things, but they make a difference in your community and enhance the well-being, if not of many, then at least of a few.

We may volunteer because we are influenced by our background. The way we engage with our local community is subject to the culture we grew up in. A person in South Africa may experience their sense of duty to their own community very differently from a French person. A Filipino may have a different idea of making their contribution to society than a New Zealander. In some places, certain actions may not even be called volunteering at all, but just represent part of our duties as members of the community.

Different cultural concepts of volunteering

It is interesting to look at the way in which volunteering is perceived in different parts of the world. The international translations of the term 'volunteering' that are interspersed throughout this book strongly reflect the cultural biases that are linked to volunteerism in different countries. For example, *bayanihan*, one of the Filipino words for 'volunteering' is made up of different components. *Bayan* means 'country', whereas *bayani* means 'hero'. *Bayanihan* means 'a number of people working together and helping each other', taken from its components, making them 'heroes for their country'.

In the Philippines, a traditional house stands on four posts and has provision for it to to be carried to another place. If a man is to marry, he will have to build a house for his wife. Should he already own a house, then he will need to move it to where the future wife currently lives. He will call upon his neighbours to help him carry. This is the visual picture of *bayanihan*, the Filipino word for volunteer service, which is, as one interviewee from the Philippines told us:

> 'Service that does not expect financial reward. Rather, because of a need, a group of people will volunteer their services to carry the house. *Bayanihan* is also recognised as a call for help. So whenever there is a crisis, a person will call for *bayanihan*, that is, volunteers. There are symbols, and stories that build on that value in the culture. So it is ingrained in the people.'

Looking at the rich heritage of African cultures, one can find a lot of concepts that define the parameters of living together. Probably the most famous of these is *ubuntu*. The term *ubuntu* originates from one of the Bantu dialects in Southern Africa and refers to a Southern African philosophy that lays out the ground rules of being part of a community.

It provides a basis of engaging with other people and stems from the belief that 'a person is a person through other people, that my humanity is caught up, bound up, inextricably, with yours'.[25] It is based on a collective rather than individual consciousness. Hospitality, respect, dignity, caring about others and a willingness to go out of one's way for someone else all find reference in *ubuntu*, deeply rooted in Southern African everyday life and applied to religion, politics and society.[26]

When talking of global citizenship, a concept such as *ubuntu* can be useful in providing guidelines as to why a global perspective matters. If we are all connected through our humanity, then it is important that we have a global perspective on our actions. What we do at home could, one day, affect a person on the other side of the planet. As a volunteer from Ghana, pointed out to us, global citizenship is 'about doing the right thing wherever you are'. If we are who we are through other people, then it is our duty to ensure the happiness of the people around us – and this will ultimately benefit us.

Often, this concept of mutuality has attracted criticism as it seems to limit the development of the individual and self-exploration to the boundaries set by the community. This may be problematic, as it could be understood that we can only ever develop within the confines of our community. If that were the case, it would stifle any attempts at development and hinder individuals from achieving their potential. But, as Nelson Mandela put it: '*Ubuntu* does not mean that people should not enrich themselves. The question therefore is: are you going to do so in order to enable the community around you to improve?' *Ubuntu* actively encourages development, but development of

THE ORIGINS OF VOLUNTEERING IN SOUTH AFRICA

Volunteerism and volunteering have always been an integral part of South Africa's rich history and traditions. What we now understand as the principles of *ilimo, letsema* (working together) and *siyasizana* (we are helping one another), these groups of individuals formed community-based self-help initiatives as well as community protest organisations to address issues related to social, political, and economic marginalisation.[27]

Subsequent to its transition to democracy, South Africa has maintained this strong heritage and many of these organisations and groups have taken the shape of formal civil society organisations and government structures. Approximately 49 per cent of the NGO sector in the country presently comprises full-time volunteers working without compensation. South Africa ranks fifth based on volunteers as a percentage of the volunteering workforce out of 28 countries.[28]

The role of volunteerism in the development of the country

Predating colonisation, the indigenous people in the Southern African region cared and shared for others living in their communities. Subsequently, a large number of organisational and volunteer groupings emerged based on the communities' need to maintain solidarity and provide basic material and spiritual support necessary for survival. Their goal was to promote and support the common good, creating a way of life that positively contributes to the well-being of a people, community and society.

To the present, many volunteers continue to provide community services in response to the gaps left by government in social services, particularly in the areas of health and social welfare. Perceptions are that government has fallen short of providing support to volunteers that provide these services as it relates to their livelihoods, i.e. health and economic stability. Where support is provided, it is neither consistent across the political geography of the country nor provided in a sustainable manner to ensure the livelihoods of volunteers.

In other cases, the contributions of volunteers are perceived by some government and donor agencies as part of the countries' cultural traditions and therefore should not involve livelihoods. However, the increased levels of poverty in South Africa have come to challenge this notion as many people use volunteerism as a medium to gain skills that help to improve their prospects for professional employment. Dialogue continues on the definitions of volunteerism and what provisions of support it should entail.

Some efforts are under way by both government and civil society to improve these measures of support. Programmes such as the National Youth Service Volunteerism Scheme as well as the grass-roots mobilisation/development of local networks in support of volunteers, are increasing steadily. In the future, more work will need to be done to raise the profile of community volunteering making it a larger part of the development discourse and resulting in direct support from government, the private sector and donor agencies.

Thabo Putu, University of the Witwatersrand, South Africa
Michael Shoenke, VSO
Ina Vermuelen, Child Welfare, Cape Town
Bella Ramos, Filipino volunteer in South Africa, Volunteer Programme Development
and Management, South Africa, 2007

a sustainable kind that increases the benefit for a community.

Another concept of collectiveness and respect for others in the rich heritage of African philosophy is the concept of *harambee*. Originating in Kenya, *harambee*, just as *ubuntu*, focuses on the ways in which individuals can work together towards the benefit of the community. The term is derived from Kiswahili language and means 'pulling together'. As a concept it is closely linked to and intertwined in Kenyan history, having become a political motto after independence in 1963, where *harambee* was used as a means to mobilise the community

DIFFERENT PLACES, DIFFERENT NAMES

Every society in the world has its own idiosyncrasies. Whether it is cultural traditions, institutions, the arts, or religion, no country will have the same diversity as another one in the world. Yet, keeping in mind these differences, intercultural comparisons between societies have still allowed us to distinguish between them along certain demarcation lines. Although these are indications or trends rather than facts set in stone, these demarcations can be useful when working and living in an intercultural context.

One such example is the way in which individuals interact with their community and the different roles that are assigned between the individual and society. Most Western countries – the liberal democracies – have placed an increasing significance on the individual within their societies and the frameworks that enable each person to develop within their own individual capacities. These societies place the individual before the community.

Other cultures have much more emphasis on community cohesion and look at the members of each community as a part of the whole, rather than seeing a community merely as the sum of its parts. A predominance of such societies can be found in Asia and Africa, with the concepts of *ubuntu* and *bayanihan* expressing a more community-oriented culture.

These cultural differences do not only have an impact on how we do certain things, they also have implications on how we refer to our actions.

Volunteering and social action are two concepts that need to be seen in such a context. Community-focused societies tend to place a lot of emphasis on what people do for each other within that community. It is expected to help out other members – there is much more social and cultural pressure on people to act when there is a need. Often in these societies, this is referred to as social action.

Individualistic societies lack this kind of expectation to act for one another. Helping others out is seen as an act of charity, a good deed. While people may lack the intrinsic impulses from within the society to act, they do it out of free will. This is what would be called volunteering.

The lesson to be learned from this is that although social action and volunteering are essentially one and the same thing – helping others without expectation of anything in return – they are rooted within different social contexts and result from different cultural settings. Different names should not, however, distract from the core of both concepts: the aim to achieve positive social change.

to raise funds for local projects and events, while government provided start-up monetary support.

Although *harambee* has become heavily criticised in recent years, owing to the political appropriation and corruption of the term, it has still helped establish and implement many development programmes for Kenya. This is because *harambee* involved people at the grass-roots level and made them give their best in order to achieve community development. In many traditional African societies, in Kenya and others, there were self-help or co-operative work groups, which organised events for members of the society. During that time, *harambee* was mainly associated with fund-raising.

Susan Chieni from Moi University in Kenya points out the four principles that make up this concept:

- a development strategy that is run mainly in a bottom-up manner
- participation is guided by mainly collective, rather than individual gain
- the felt needs of the majority should guide the choice of projects
- project implementation should maximise the use of local resources. [29]

These principles represent much of what the modern notion of volunteering is based on. Making a difference in a local community and involving the local community is the groundwork of volunteering and social action.

Bayanihan, *ubuntu* and *harambee* all demonstrate the ways in which our culture can affect the manner in which we engage with the community around us. Where these concepts in a community prevail, volunteering is part and parcel of everyday life, although it may not be called volunteering as such. Community service, duty and helping others were among the descriptions of voluntary actions on the local level; the levels of engagement differ greatly in different parts of the world.

Most liberal democracies stress the individual more than the community, which is why volunteering in those places tends to be more institutionalised, thus more visible. Community-oriented societies will be less formal about the ways that they help others.

Religion

Cultural concepts of community, as we have seen, can be pervasive in the way we relate to the people around us. Although there are great global variations, the community will always feature to greater or lesser extents in our perception. Every society has its own concept of community. Besides cultural concepts of living together, religion or spirituality also matter to most communities around the world.

Religion has been a strong driver for volunteerism throughout its history. As already mentioned in Chapter 1, the Golden Rule, which most religions are based on, is one of reciprocity. Do not do to others, what you don't want done to yourself. Or, alternatively, do to others what you would like others to do for you. Many rites of religion include charity and helping others.

The commandment of 'Love thy neighbour' requires Christians to be benevolent to others. One of the five Pillars of Islam, *zakat*, makes it a commandment for Muslims to give to the poor. It is a tax that is levied in proportion – 2.5 per cent – of a person's income and wealth. As the majority of the Islamic countries have adopted Western fiscal policy, this tax is mainly voluntary. Paid by large numbers in the community, it goes towards charitable causes as laid down in the Qu'ran. According to Islam, the poor are to be treated with respect and it is a duty for a good Muslim to share some of his food and material belongings with a person that is worse off. Giving money to the poor is seen as a vital part of everyday life.

In Germany, the largest help campaign by children is called *Sternsinger* and is organised by the Catholic Church. Every year, around the Epiphany, a Christian festival celebrated on 6 January, which commemorates the first manifestation of Jesus to the Gentiles, as represented by the Magi, children volunteer to dress up as Casper, Melchior and Balthazar and go from door to door in their local community to bless the houses and sing for the inhabitants, at the same time asking, in return, for donations that go towards charitable causes for children worldwide. These are then invested globally into building kindergartens, schools, youth centres or other facilities from which the receiving children can benefit.

Church-related volunteering has received much criticism over recent years, as it is seen as a charitable function that is targeting symptoms without addressing the cause of suffering. Charity as a concept is a very old term. In an essay called 'The Concept of Unselfish Service', Emory S. Bogardus (US sociologist, 1882–1973) gives a historical analysis of different terms associated with welfare in the broadest sense. According to this historical study, the term charity has undergone a fall from grace. While it used to be seen as a genuine act of generosity, it has come to carry more selfish connotations.

'Charity was once highly honoured; it connoted the supreme principle of love. It came, however, to refer to the dispensing of alms with one hand, while the donor was receiving with the other hand large sums of unearned income.'[30] These days, charity has been seen to fail to meet

Okwehayo
Giving your time/self
UGANDA

FAILA PAŠIĆ BIŠIĆ
'The best volunteer in Slovenia', 2006

Islam is a religion that cares for the welfare of all humans and calls for participating in volunteer activities and services for people without awaiting any reward from them. In this sense volunteering is deeply rooted in Islamic teachings and practices. In Islam, doing voluntary acts to help others is not restricted to a certain race or religion but it encompasses all human beings and even all creatures.

Every voluntary act by a Muslim to bring about a material benefit or happiness for a human being is regarded as an act of worship. Islam designates several forms of social services as kinds of charity: removing a harmful thing from the road or street, enjoining what is good, reconciling two people, receiving someone with a smile, a good word, and so on.

Volunteering refers to doing an activity of one's own will and without being paid for it or without expecting any material reward for it. As for Muslims, they are strongly recommended to do many volunteer acts and they should do so.

Volunteering is my lifeblood, because it allows me to do so much. I can run organisations, provide social services, organise conferences, set up playgroups and drop-in centres, feed the hungry, shelter the homeless, run schools and set up blood banks. The list could go on.

In 2006, I received the award of 'best volunteer in Slovenia' for my activities. This was for several volunteer programmes that I contributed to or organised. These were a therapeutic programme run by volunteer family therapists providing support to families and their children with a focus on strengthening families, especially asylum seekers, and a radio programme called *Giving voice to the voiceless*. I also helped provide accommodation, and education and, with that, contributed to a better quality of life for the children of Srebrenica and supported projects that helped the poor and disabled in Slovenia and set up humanitarian concerts for orphans.

In order to motivate volunteers, you have to be motivated yourself. I'm always trying to show the volunteers what the 'face' of success looks like in their activities. A key to motivating volunteers is focusing on the successes of their work and to show the difference they have made to another person. In volunteering, you have to be ready to always expect the unexpected.

I try to promote love, peace, brotherhood, tolerance and understanding among all nations, cultures, races and religions of the world. The 'one world' concept should come into existence if we are to ensure a peaceful coexistence for our future generations.

For my beloved volunteers, for myself

Faila

PROFILE

49

the demands of our current problems. More is needed than the pure provision of consumables in order to make a difference.

But at the same time, all major world religions promote welfare and caring for others. The Parliament of the World's Religions is a regular meeting, which brings together more than 600 church officials from the world religions to discuss the promotion of a peaceful and sustainable world. Since 1988, the Parliament has met every five years with over 8,000 people from all over the world coming to contribute to the mission of making this world a better place by trying to replace religious and cultural hatred with the celebration of diversity and harmony. The size of the conference shows the major impact that religion can have on people's lives.[31]

A volunteer from New Zealand, whom we interviewed, said that to her religion was a strong impetus to volunteer: 'I think that religion can definitely play a part. If you look at all the world religions they are all based on respect for other people and to do unto others as you would have them do to you.'

Personal reasons

Of course, cultural concepts and differences alone cannot account for the vast number of people who have decided to give their time and energy to volunteering. We have already looked at the way certain volunteers have different qualifications and expectations they take into their volunteering experience. As varied as personalities are the benefits people get from volunteering. There are as many motivations for volunteering as there are volunteering opportunities. They include the desire 'to give something back'; meeting new people; making a positive contribution; wanting to have fun; and 'wanting to get something out of it'.

Often, the reasons for volunteering are a mix of different factors. In some cases, a particular event can be the trigger for us to get involved in volunteering, as the following story from a Ghanaian interviewee shows:

'After studying, I worked as a maintenance engineer at a company. While I was there, I was also in charge of paying the allowances of the workers and quite often I misappropriated the money. I did not pay the right amount to the workers and I kept some of it. I discovered this organisation that was talking about ethical values and it struck me that, when I was a student leader I led all sorts of campaigns against corruption while I was in the polytechnic, and realised I was corrupt now, even

RELIGION AND VOLUNTEERING

Religion can be a strong motivation for volunteers. All religions are based on concepts of reciprocity and helping each other, especially the less privileged. Whether *zakat*, the Muslim principle of giving to the poor, the Golden Rule for Christians: 'Do to others what you would have them do to you' or the dictum: 'Never impose on others what you would not choose for yourself' in Confucianism, they all encourage supporting others.

At the same time, religious conflicts erupt around the world. Confrontations based on religion are nothing new: the Reformation, missionary expeditions to colonies, anti-Semitism or the Troubles in Northern Ireland all express perceived differences around faith. Although many countries have moved towards secularism, religion still creates a strong backdrop to conflict. The most obvious examples are the religious tensions after America's 9/11 and the London bombings of July 2007. Suicide bombings in the name of religion and a rise in general mistrust between members of people of different religious groups are manifestations of the new era in which religion, or radical forms thereof, has come to strongly affect peace and intercultural understanding. Even the Israeli–Palestinian conflict, although not essentially rooted in religion, comes with issues relating to the use of religious monuments by both Muslims and Jews.

These conflicts, based on a distorted sense of religious belonging, pose a threat to international negotiations. While governments are struggling to find solutions on how to resolve conflicts and break down barriers and prejudice based around religion, more and more people suffer from the consequences of a spiralling course of events.

Volunteering can be a way of tackling rising suspicion and mistrust and of actively promoting interfaith dialogue and co-operation.

The southern region of Mindanao in the Philippines is home to the second oldest internal conflict in the world, going back to the 16th century, when Spanish colonisers came to the Philippines and attempted to convert the Islamist island of Mindanao to Catholicism. Although relatively quiet after independence of the Philippines in 1948, there was a resurgence of violent clashes in the 1960s owing to a resentment by the Muslim majority towards central control and an increasing number of Christian settlers. The roots of the conflict are essentially over land rights and natural resources, but religious differences have still strongly shaped the ways in which the conflict emerged.[32] It has been the centre of numerous, albeit unsuccessful, peace negotiations and preoccupied Filipino politicians and activists as well as international diplomats.

The Muslim volunteering organisation Kapamagogopa Inc. (K.I.), which translates as 'Muslims sharing skills for peace and development', was founded to positively change the five-century-old conflict in Mindanao, which has taken more than 120,000 lives already. K.I. was set up to provide professional opportunities for young Muslim adults, giving them the chance to break social isolation and to work in multicultural environments; to support the professional development of young Muslim adults, who are eager to voice the rights of self-determination of Muslims in the Philippines; to break the stereotype of Muslims who are seen as recipients with no or little recognition of their skills or contribution to development and peace building; to assign skilled local volunteers to areas of Mindanao and other parts of the country where international volunteers have limited access because of cultural and/or security concerns; and to develop a holistic approach to the peace process with international and local techniques and methods in areas where both local and international volunteers are present.

The volunteers involved with K.I. are 20- to 27-year-old Muslim professionals, who speak English, Filipino (Tagalog), one common dialect and one ethnic dialect, and have a knowledge of the basic tenets of Islam. These young men and women work together to bring equal opportunities, development and most of all peace to the region of Mindanao. They are placed with various organisations ranging from governmental agencies, to community-based groups and co-operatives. There they run workshops, teach and engage people in the themes of capacity-building, gender sensitivity and spiritual and moral education. The main focus of the work is on improving Muslim–Christian relations through reconciliation, emotional and psycho-social recovery, improving access to health and sanitation, and developing micro-livelihoods by using sustainable natural resource management. By looking at the causes of poverty, K.I. hopes to overcome Christian–Muslim conflicts in the area. K.I.'s work can be a way of overcoming negative perceptions of some Muslims not just for the Philippines, but also worldwide. Musa Sanguila, a member of K.I.'s Board of Trustees, sums up the conviction of K.I. in the idea that 'there is no such thing as a Christian–Muslim issue. We share the same problems and we are confronted by the same challenges, especially when we talk of peace.'

Robby Nazal, from VSO Bahaginan, an organisation that was instrumental in the setting up of K.I. also sees volunteering as a way of overcoming misconceptions between people both within the region, but also in the world:

'Volunteering can potentially bring about inspiration to change, to break down barriers. Volunteering can help break down the myths in the area that Muslims are the recipients of development and the source of the conflict by showing the real issues behind the conflict, which are not only religion-based, but also revolve around land possessions and conflict between indigenous clans. If both national and international volunteers are placed in a community in Mindanao, it will change the world's perception. As long as volunteers stay, it is a way of battling perceptions.'

though I was doing it on a much smaller scale. I began to reflect on what I should or what I could do, and that is when my volunteer work started.'

Some people volunteer, because to them it is fun. They enjoy meeting new people, experiencing new cultures and doing something different to their everyday routines. In our interviews, people have said that volunteering helped them to get to know themselves better. By doing something that is out of their comfort zone, they felt as though they were learning about their own abilities as well as limitations. A heightened self-awareness together with the feeling of doing something worthwhile can be a real boost to a person's self-confidence. It makes people feel relevant.

Also, many people volunteer when they have come to a dead end in their lives and they feel that they need to change something about themselves. This can be purely personal, but in many parts of the world, volunteering can also be regarded as a way of starting a second career. It allows the volunteer to try out something new, without putting performance pressure on the individual, as their work is voluntary. They do not need to meet stringently articulated levels of performance as they would in other sectors of work. Because they do something voluntarily, they feel that people will recognise their goodwill and be less likely to judge them purely according to performance measurement frameworks.

Different motives, powerful solutions

In the Western world, a tendency towards a more individualistic and acquisitive lifestyle has raised severe doubts about the levels of social cohesion and individual well-being in the years ahead. Reasons for alienation and anxiety include longer work hours, pressures on meeting performance levels, lack of time, and so on. Governments in these countries are beginning to realise that for individuals and for families, volunteering can provide a way of socialising that is also a healing remedy for fragmented and divided societies.

Nakyena
Volunteer free will
UGANDA

The examples from this chapter have shown how our sociocultural background can influence our involvement in volunteering. Some may see volunteering as a sacrifice, others as a duty and then again others as a way of contributing to their community. Some may want to give something back out of gratitude; others may volunteer out of guilt. All these form a strong interplay between what motivates us on a personal level, which societal structures enhance involvement and how individual and community interact. Regardless of motivation, it is the fundamental desire to become involved that is paramount.

The most successful volunteering organisations will be those who keep all these issues in mind. In our next chapter, we look at the strategic choices for volunteering organisations in today's complex, interdependent world of volunteering.

WHY DO YOU VOLUNTEER?

To make a contribution to the community

'The idea of belonging to and being an active member of one's community is very important to a lot of people. They feel a particular affinity with and responsibility for the neighbourhood in which they live and with the people with whom they share; like citizenship, but on a smaller scale. This in turn feeds into desire to contribute to its development, to enrich it, and the lives of those who live there. Your community may well have given a lot to you and you feel the need to give something back in return.'

To make a positive change

'Many people have either experienced the benefits of volunteer-based projects or can see the necessity for them across a whole range of fields. Having identified areas of need and areas of potential, they then feel sufficiently empowered to be able to become agents of that change, with the only reward being a feeling of satisfaction at actually having made a difference. One person alone can't make a huge impact, but when volunteers work together as agents of change, the sky's the limit. People see this and want to be part of it.'

To feel relevant

'The world can sometimes seem a big and lonely place in which individuals and their actions are so insignificant as to be virtually invisible. The opportunity to actually feel as though you matter, and that your actions are relevant to the lives of others is a very strong motivation for many people, giving a feeling of empowerment and satisfaction that might hitherto have been lacking.'

To help others

'There isn't a person in the world who has never needed somebody's help at some point in their lives and therefore each and every one of us knows how wonderful it is when someone is there for us. Many people volunteer specifically because the work they do brings them directly into contact with people who need help, and moreover because they, the volunteers, know that they are in the position to give it. The knowledge that their actions have helped someone else and the satisfaction that that brings is the greatest reward possible.'

Religious motivations

'Good deeds, love, and respect for those around us is central to the vast majority of religions. Whether the motivation comes from the idea of reciprocity (what Christians would articulate as "do to others as you would have them do to you"), the promise of reward in the afterlife, or the sanctity of inner spiritual fulfilment, there has long been a tradition of religious followers engaging in a wide range of volunteering activities, both within, and outside of their individual faith communities.'

Guilt and atonement

'Guilt has any number of roots and still more ways in which it manifests itself. One of these ways is in the desire to atone for one's perceived wrongs by putting aside consideration of one's own self and one's own comforts. Those experiencing feelings of guilt often feel that they deserve no reward for what they are doing and wish to convince both themselves and/or others, that they can make up for past actions by helping people in as selfless a way as is deemed possible. On a broader note, guilt could also be rooted in an awareness of the inequalities of the world and the guilt of privilege that one may feel one does not deserve or only has by an accident of birth.'

For the 'experience'

'There's a certain romance attached to the idea of volunteering. For many it's a personal journey of self-discovery that profoundly changes the way they think about themselves and view the world as a whole. Testimonies abound, from people describing just how much volunteering has enriched their lives and opened their eyes to the world. Human nature is such that if something is described as fulfilling, exciting, and an unforgettable experience, we are naturally attracted to it and wish to experience it ourselves.'

Because I reached a stage in my career where I wanted to change and get out of the rat race

'A lot gets said about the stresses and strains of living in a 24/7 global society. At times it seems as if the world is moving so fast that we just get swept along and lose sight of what's important among the endless targets, e-mails, reports, projections and seemingly pointless stationary ordering procedures. Sometimes we just need to stop and take a step back and re-evaluate our lives, and volunteering is a way that some people seek to do this, removing themselves from the rat race and seeking out something more fulfilling to apply their energies to.'

I didn't know what I wanted to do

'The pressure to choose a career is often felt by young people nearing the end of their education. Many people go straight from school or university into the job market and often struggle to find a job that they are suited to. Provided that you are in a position to do so, volunteering is an excellent way to spend a few months or a year assessing your situation and making a more informed decision about your future. You can apply what skills you possess, learn new ones, and, simply put, emerge in a far better position to make the big decisions that will shape the rest of your life.'

Passion

'For some people, the desire to help people, to get involved, and the desire to make a difference goes way beyond simple satisfaction but actually develops into a full-blown passion. Volunteering becomes a paramount defining characteristic of that individual and a *raison d'être*. Volunteering excites them, fulfils them, and quite frankly, there's nothing else they would rather be doing. The very success of many projects hinges on the passion of an individual and the difference that this kind of dedication can make is immense.'

To gain experience/skills and as a stepping stone to bigger things

'Breaking into the job market, particularly into certain areas, can be very difficult without experience relevant to the job. Volunteering is a very common way in which people attempt to gain job-related skills that will enhance their value in the job market. They are then able to better position themselves to be able to apply for work in certain sectors, particularly the not-for-profit sector.

Even if the career you desire does not specifically relate to the volunteer work in which you have been engaged, the qualities and skills displayed, such as teamwork, flexibility, initiative, dedication, interpersonal skills and cross-cultural experience, are viewed extremely favourably by prospective employers and will inevitably enhance a CV.'

Community pressure

'Some communities engage in high levels of collective volunteer work. In many cases, joining in with this and being seen to be actively contributing is an important part of gaining acceptance. Rightly or wrongly, this is a compelling motivation for a number of people to become involved and does build up a sense of identity that has a significant impact on the person's life.'

It becomes addictive

'Once you get involved with volunteer projects and once you feel the energy, the satisfaction and the "buzz", it can be a very difficult thing to stop. Although there are multiple reasons why people *begin* to volunteer in the first place, when it comes to why people *continue*, the field narrows somewhat. The truth is that people like it, it makes them feel good, and once they have finished one thing, they find themselves immediately looking around for the next. It can become a craving not totally dissimilar to that of nicotine, the only difference being this is one addiction you won't want to give up.'

A way to fill employment gaps

'Throughout one's working life it is not uncommon to experience periods out of employment, whether this be voluntary or otherwise. What many people like to do is to use this time to carry out voluntary work that, as well as filling time that might otherwise have been spent idly, contributes positively to society and also can equip the volunteer with skills, contacts, and other opportunities to find paid employment in the future.'

To feel good by doing good

'Make no mistake about it, volunteering, helping people, doing something for others and for no material gain, can feel good. A lot of people don't care about *why* they do it, they just know that it makes them feel good. And sometimes there really is no need to look beyond that.'

Friendship

'When people meet on volunteering projects, be it over a day, a week or a year, they form friendships that can last for the rest of their lives. There's something about living and working in close proximity, about striving for a common purpose, that brings out the best in people and that brings them closer together. It is also an opportunity to move outside of your normal circle, and to meet new people from different backgrounds and with different experiences to share.'

To learn more about other people's cultures

'Curiosity and a desire to expand one's knowledge about the world around us is a human characteristic that we all possess on one level or another. One of the fabulous things about volunteering is that it brings us into contact with different groups outside of our normal walk of life. Learning about other people's cultures, about the situations they face, the traditions and customs that permeate their lives, forms an integral part of all kinds of volunteer work, be it on the other side of the world, or within your own towns and cities.'

Personal associations

'What brings many people into volunteering activities is a personal connection with the participants in the project, scheme or initiative in which they become involved. Parents frequently give their time to run scout groups, sports teams and other extra-curricular activities, for example. Similarly, charity volunteers often choose charities that tackle issues that have personally affected them and those closest to them and this brings an integrity and sincerity of purpose otherwise missing from their lives. Any volunteering initiative will be greatly strengthened by the presence of deeply held personal convictions.'

HIGHLIGHTS AND CHALLENGES OF INTERNATIONAL VOLUNTEERING

On a rainy day in February, we met with four young volunteers on Global Xchange. The team had come back from three months in Lafia, Nigeria, to complete a three-month volunteer placement in Brighton, in the UK. Gwennan Roberts is from North Wales and has just finished a degree in sociolinguistics and wanted to volunteer abroad. Megan Hood is from Edinburgh. She has not been to university yet and was at a stage where she did not know what she wanted to do with her life, so she thought doing a programme like this would be really useful. She used to volunteer in Oxfam before she joined Global Xchange. Kareem Folajaiye from Nigeria has also just finished secondary school and was waiting for admission to university for two years. He saw the Global Xchange opportunity and decided to volunteer. Adam Galadima is from the northern part of Nigeria. He had just finished school and had a whole year to do whatever he chose to do, so he chose to volunteer with Global Xchange. The young volunteers had been on the programme for four months, and in Brighton for just over a month. We talked about the Global Xchange experience and the highlights and challenges of volunteering.

Aurélie Bröckerhoff

Tell me about your Global Xchange experience. You have been here for four weeks now.

Megan Hood

Yes, but we have been on the programme for four months because we started in September and we spent three months in Nigeria, which everyone found very challenging but, at the same time, very rewarding.

Aurélie Bröckerhoff

How was your experience in Nigeria?

Megan Hood

For me, it was a very big culture shock. The place we were in was very rural and very different from my hometown. Being there alone was very challenging but the fact that we knew we were making a difference helped in a way, because we knew we were doing something good and the community really benefited from us being there. Just walking down the street made their day because we were there for them.

Aurélie Bröckerhoff

What kind of work did you do?

Megan Hood

We did a great deal of road-safety work because the town did not really have safety rules. They did not wear helmets when they went on motorbikes and they did not really have a speed limit, and no traffic lights because of a lack of electricity. So we thought that it would be a good idea to join with schoolchildren and do road-safety rallies and talk to the community about wearing helmets, slowing down, and just being more careful on the roads because while we were there we did see a lot of accidents. We thought it was an important issue to tackle.

Aurélie Bröckerhoff

What impact and influence did you have?

Megan Hood

We did actually see more people wearing helmets by the end of the three months, but when I say 'more', it was three or four people rather than none. I think we did make an impact but I do not know whether or not it will carry on.

Gwennan Roberts

It was very challenging but, at the same time, I felt good that I had managed to spend three months in a place that was so different from home. Even for the people from Nigeria, it was really different because it was so rural. While we were there, there were three major international days. There was World Aids Day, International Volunteer Day, and World Disability Day, and we did projects on all three of those days. We did an especially big one on World Aids Day, where we did a rally, teaching people how to use condoms and things like that. It was good.

Adam Galadima

For me, it was also very challenging because it was different from the community where I come from. It was very hot and it was a rural area. We worked with the Family Health Care Foundation, where they were dealing with HIV and Aids. I think we made a tremendous impact because we were able to put people through testing and counselling. When we had our World Aids Day, most people came for the testing and it was because the volunteers were there. We were able to motivate people to get tested.

Kareem Folajaiye

It was a challenging experience for me as well, I would say, because I worked with a YMCA [Young Men's Christian Association] and in the town where we were, Lafia, there were many HIV-positive children. I remember we had a workshop with the Institute of Human Virology from Abuja, where they came and talked to us about health care for vulnerable children who live with people who have Aids or other deadly diseases. I learned so much, while I was helping, so that has been a great experience for me.

Aurélie Bröckerhoff

What was it like living with a counterpart? Did it help or was it really complicated at the start?

Megan Hood

It is not complicated so much as just challenging because I think all the Nigerians and the UK people are very different, especially culturally. We each have our own way of doing things, as any two people would, but it is just that little bit more challenging because it is someone that may not understand you as well or just may not understand the way you do things. Because we all speak English, we do not have that language barrier, but there are still communication issues – the ways that we say and do things – and, therefore, it can be quite challenging at times.

Adam Galadima

To me it was challenging as well, but not that much because I knew we were coming from different backgrounds and with different cultural values. So if you try as much as possible to understand the person and whatever he or she does, they will not look on it as an attack. You try to look at what it really is, try to understand it, and then you usually do not have a problem.

Aurélie Bröckerhoff

What were the highlights of your experience in Nigeria?

Gwennan Roberts

We had a weekend in the middle of each of the three months to go away from the community to a place called Jos. It was so much fun; we had such a good time. We had an unexpectedly good time because we always complain about another week of training, but this was fun and Jos was so much colder. It was a laugh.

Megan Hood

For me, just meeting completely different people and learning from them was quite rewarding in itself, and realising things that I would not have, if I had not had the experience. For example that I took simple things, like running water, for granted.

Adam Galadima

And constant electricity.

Megan Hood

Yes, I really take constant electricity for granted – being able to walk into a room and switch on the light. Without having to worry about the fact that it is too hot and the fan will not go or it is too dark and I want to read but there is no light. I do not take things for granted as much as I used to and I am really glad about this. I appreciate everything that I have.

Aurélie Bröckerhoff

What is it like here in the UK? Are there different challenges or highlights?

Adam Galadima

Yes. Here in the UK it is entirely different. First, we talk about the weather. It is very cold and challenging for the Nigerian volunteers. Also, the way things are done out in Nigeria are completely different from the way things are done here in the UK – there is more paperwork here, for example. In Nigeria, you can come and say, 'I am a volunteer', and no one will ask you for any ID or official documentation, but here even looking for a volunteer placement is kind of a challenge. So there are little challenges. Things are not done easily out here compared with the way they are in Nigeria, so it is a challenge.

Megan Hood

But then when we went to Nigeria we found it very challenging to do things. We were trying to do it our way because we thought that was the best way to do it and it just was not and it did not work. It took us a while to realise that we had to adapt our way – just simple things like wanting to meet someone to talk to them or interview them. We would send them a letter and expect a reply but the letter did not get there for a week and we wanted to talk to them the next day, so it was just very challenging for us and they found it challenging because it is the opposite way for them to do things.

Adam Galadima

One nice thing about that is even though in Nigeria you might send a letter and it does not get there straight away, as soon as the person receives the letter, things can get done in two hours, if it's something really urgent.

Kareem Folajaiye

There is a disadvantage to that. Everything is last minute. So it does not really give you time to plan anything.

Adam Galadima

That is what I have learned on Global Xchange – how to plan and do things under pressure.

Kareem Folajaiye

On Global Xchange, we have experienced a lot of diversity in the team and in the programme as well – two different communities, two different ways of doing things – so it is a new experience. Here in the UK, so much is different. The way people express themselves and approach you, the way they ask for things or the way they give is different. Even just greeting people and meeting up is totally different from how it is here. I am glad that I am on Global Xchange because if I had come here just on my own, without my counterpart and without the Global Xchange experience, it would have been harder for me to carry out some of the things that I am doing now.

With the help of my counterpart and other people from Global Xchange, I have been able to learn more about the culture and how people see and do things. I now know more about the culture and how to act, so I will not step on someone's toes.

Gwennan Roberts

Also, in the UK, especially for young people, there is a great deal of emphasis on volunteering abroad in supposedly less-fortunate countries, but with Global Xchange, you get the chance to volunteer at home as well. There are places in the UK that need volunteers too and one of the good things about Global Xchange is that is halves the time between the UK and whichever country.

Adam Galadima

No matter how developed the UK is, there are many problems. Back home, people just think that the UK or most of the developed countries are problem-free. As we have come here and volunteered, we have seen that there are still problems to be tackled. We cannot say that there are not problems because it is a developed country.

Megan Hood

When I told people about the programme and said that I would be spending three months in a developing country and then three months in the UK, they asked: 'Why are you spending three months in the UK?' The UK still has problems; it still needs volunteers. It is just that because we are a developed country it is not thought that it is needed as much, but it *is* still needed. Just because it is not as obvious or in-your-face, the UK will still benefit a great deal from volunteers.

Endnotes

[23] Kant, Immanuel (1990) *The Metaphysics of Morals*, Cambridge University Press

[24] A good summary of the study and perception of stereotypes is the essay 'A Theory of Stereotypes' by Forrest LaViolette and K.H. Silvert. In: *Social Forces*, vol. 29, no. 3, March 1951, University of North Carolina Press

[25] Desmond Tutu: www.cyc-net.org/today2000/today000328.html

[26] www.buzzle.com/editorials/7-22-2006-103206.asp

[27] VSO-NDA, Reference Group, Terms of Reference, August 2006

[28] Social Surveys, 'The Size and Scope of the Non-Profit Sector in South Africa', 1999

[29] For a detailed discussion of *harambee*: Chieni, Susan, Njeri, 'The Harambee Movement in Kenya. The Role Played by Kenyans and the Government in the Provision of Education and other Social Services', Moi University, Kenya: http://boleswa97.tripod.com/chieni.htm

[30] 'The concept of unselfish service': Emory S. Bogardus, *Journal of Social Forces*, vol. 1, no. 2, University of North Carolina Press, January 1923, pp. 100–102, used by permission of the publisher

[31] www.cpwr.org

[32] For a more detailed view on the Mindanao conflict: Schiavo-Campo, Salvatore & Judd, Mary, 'The Mindanao Conflict in the Philippines: Roots, Costs, and Potential Peace Dividend', *Social Development Papers: Conflict Prevention and Reconstruction*, paper no. 24, The World Bank, February 2005

CHAPTER 3

HOW TO GET INVOLVED

'I am not a liberator.
Liberators do not exist.
The people liberate
themselves.'

ERNESTO CHE GUEVARA, 1928–67

Global Xchange volunteer, James, doing daily chores with host brother, Lennox, in Malawi. © Simon Rawles/VSO

HOW TO GET INVOLVED

We have talked about the motivations of and reasons why people volunteer. But once the decision to get involved has been made, what next?

We need to remember what we mean by the term volunteering: giving your time, energy, love – in short, something of yourself – to someone or something else, without expecting any rewards in return. This could be preparing some food for the people in your office or helping a friend move. Without recognising them as such, we all probably engage in voluntary actions several times a day – taking photographs at our neighbour's birthday party, or posting a letter for someone. All these represent actions for which we do not expect any return.

What all these have in common is the fact that the recipient is someone we have a personal relationship with. But as we have already mentioned, people often also help those whom they don't know – giving someone directions, helping an old lady on to a bus or offering our seat to someone who needs it more than we do. These reflect on basic altruistic principles that are engrained in every one of us as a result of our social nature. We rarely ask ourselves why we do these things; they seem natural, and we feel in some ways a connection, a responsibility to the other person.

But can all of this alone account for the overall rise of volunteering worldwide? People have always had friends who wrote letters, neighbours have always had birthdays and foreigners were never sure of directions. Pure altruism doesn't explain why an increasing number of people spend their time working in soup kitchens, campaigning for global justice or travel overseas to help build houses for the less fortunate.

One of the reasons that more and more people become volunteers has been outlined in Chapter 1. Through the process of globalisation, we feel more connected with the world around us. We cannot disassociate ourselves from the wider structures of a global framework. Chapter 2 looked at the motivations we can have for volunteering, which ranged from personal traits to cultural or social concepts that enable a tradition of volunteering within certain societies.

Another major reason for the increase in volunteering is the rising availability of opportunities to be involved. Some may argue that this

Kuthandiza
Helping
ZAMBIA

is because modernity has led to an increasing number of issues that need to be addressed by volunteers. Others may say that modernity has increased awareness of what needs to be done to achieve global betterment. But whatever one's own viewpoint is, it is undeniable that there are rising numbers of more or less structured approaches of being involved.

Volunteering organisations

Although volunteering can be done on the individual level, as the above examples show, often people will turn to volunteering organisations, who can help them in finding appropriate voluntary work in an area that interests them.

Turning to volunteering organisations has several advantages. First, they can assist in the preparation for the volunteering experience and teach the volunteer the dos and don'ts of the volunteering experience. Second, these organisations usually possess a large framework of like-minded people who can exchange ideas and share experiences with each other. This can help the volunteers reflect on their own experience and learn from it. Third, these organisations are specialised in volunteering and experts on the issues surrounding it and can therefore optimise the benefit of the volunteering experience for both the volunteer and the recipient.

Volunteering organisations have the role of 'gatekeeper' between volunteering opportunity and the individual who wants to become involved. They focus on areas identified as important, for example fighting poverty, stopping the spread of HIV and Aids and other diseases, climate change or education. Volunteers will approach them if they are interested in and passionate about the cause that the volunteering organisation is representing. John Watson, Programme Director, Amnesty International Scotland, told us: 'Commitment to the cause is the principal reason for volunteers to engage with a particular organisation; the organisations also need to ensure that the volunteers have something interesting to do and are able to feel that they are making a real contribution.'

Volunteering organisations come in many forms and guises. They can be governmental, non-governmental, religious or politically motivated. They operate on a local, national, international or supranational level. In terms of strategy, volunteering organisations can operate through both direct and indirect intervention, show physical or online presence, work at the grass-roots level or originate from the top. They range from 'one-man shows' to major organisations with hundreds of employees all over the world.

> **Wantokism**
>
> Helping people who speak the same language
> PAPUA NEW GUINEA

They cover themes ranging from acting to zoo-keeping. They aim at helping – the poor, the old, the disabled, the environment, socially excluded groups and so on.

Volunteering can be accessed at every level in society. Although the third sector, the non-profit, non-governmental sector, is traditionally seen as the home turf of volunteering, volunteering has also become increasingly visible in the public and private sectors. The public sector is a non-profit sector, which is regulated by governments and funded by public taxation. Much volunteering can be done in the public sector, for example in museums, schools and libraries. In a survey undertaken by Johns Hopkins University into non-profit organisations, data were collected from 36 countries and showed that volunteering accounts for 44 per cent of work hours in this area, which represents an average 1.6 per cent of the total labour force in these countries (2.7 per cent in the developed countries). This is a lot considering that, on average, only about ten per cent of the adult population of these countries participated in any volunteering activities at all.[33] In recent years though, volunteering has not been restricted to non-profit organisations; the private sector has also seen a rise in volunteering as more and more corporations have policies to support volunteering by their staff.

Specific circumstances

Often, volunteering organisations arise out of a specific set of circumstances. Oxfam was established in Europe during the Second

World War with a plan to alleviate famine by sending food to the Greek people, ignoring the Allied blockade that isolated Greece. Similarly, Amnesty International was founded after human rights violations in dictatorial Portugal under António Salazar in the early 1960s prompted a British lawyer to take action. Médecins Sans Frontières (Doctors without Borders), the world's largest international medical relief agency, was set up in 1971, a time when political and economic upheaval shook most of the world, South American countries struggled with their newly found independence and the Vietnam War filled the agenda of news, media and everyday life.

It is the same story for SAMIGOS, a South African volunteering organisation, with the aim to strengthen the ties of friendship and understanding between the people of South Africa and Mozambique through dialogue, exchange and action, and by recognising the historical, geographic, social, economic and cultural links that exist between the two countries.

Mozambique gained independence from Portugal in 1975. As with many of Portugal's ex-colonies, the new government was inspired by the Socialist movement and gave support to neighbouring anti-colonialist and anti-apartheid groups – the African National Congress (ANC) and Zimbabwe African National Union (ZANU). By fighting apartheid, Mozambique suffered financially and socially because South Africa partly financed the Mozambican National Resistance (RENAMO), an organisation dedicated to undermining the new government through armed combat. This led to hostility between both countries.

After severe floods hit Central and Southern Mozambique in February 2000, a group of people dedicated to both Mozambique and South Africa formed SAMIGOS – the South African–Mozambique Friendship Association. Although initially formed to provide assistance and help in the aftermath of the floods, the organisation was also committed to recognising the affinity that South Africa and Mozambique share. It is through community projects that SAMIGOS has worked

Доброволци
(Dobrovolci)
Goodwill
BULGARIA

to overcome hurdles to the recognition of this close relationship.

SAMIGOS runs a successful student exchange and volunteer programme between the two countries, allowing students to converge on development projects. These exchanges allow students to develop a deeper understanding of the issues that affect both South Africa and Mozambique as well as gain valuable organisational and developmental skills.

Similarly, Pravah, which is a non-profit organisation in New Delhi, works with adolescents and youth organisations to promote social justice. It was established in 1992, when a group of young professionals responded to the demolition of the Babri Masjid mosque in Ayodhya, India – destroyed as a result of political and religious tensions. The conflict that led to the demolition is still not entirely resolved, but the wave of communal riots and bloodshed that followed before and after the event are still remembered. At that time, the founders of Pravah mobilised public opinion against the violence by means of campaigns and other creative activity.

Pravah's name means flow – 'the free *flow* of knowledge, ideas, experiences and expressions among people to bring about change; the flow also represents the life journey of every individual from self to society'. This concept epitomises their work and is a basis for their programmes, which aim to help develop an understanding of social issues and dispel stereotypes. Ashraf Patel launched Pravah to help young people break out of the structures of society, develop themselves and address social issues through dance, drama, educational programmes and community work.

One of their programmes is Smile – the Students Mobilisation Initiative for Learning through Exposure – and it provides opportunities for young people to learn about social issues by working with disadvantaged people, visiting rural non-governmental organisations and by using theatre and research groups. With Making Changemakers, Pravah has also developed a citizenship, education and life-skills curriculum for schools. To support young people in becoming active global citizens, they have set up a website – www.younginfluencers.com – which provides a source of information. Another programme initiated by Pravah is Campaigns, an annual creative action programme that allows young people to co-operate with activists on current social campaigns.

These examples illustrate how at times of need, volunteering organisations tend to be set up to help address these immediate issues. They register a desire to not just engage on the individual level, but collectively. They also recognise that some issues just cannot be

> **Добровольческая служба**
> Goodwill service
> RUSSIA

PRAVAH

Pravah is an Indian organisation working with adolescents to promote social justice. It was founded to address the issues raised by the demolition of the Babri Masjid mosque in Ayodhya, in December 1992, and has since helped young people develop themselves and society through dance, drama, educational programmes and community work.

www.pravah.org
www.younginfluencers.com

addressed individually but will require uniting our efforts and strengths in order to improve situations. One of the reasons for this is the understanding that the events that prompt direct action are usually connected to wider structural deficiencies in a system.

Cyclone Larry destroyed most of Australia's banana harvests in northern Queensland in 2006, which plunged the banana industry into a deep crisis in the country. Yet, apart from sending banana prices for those available through the roof and harming the income of Queensland farmers, this incident did not lead to major societal problems. This is because there was a system in place to ensure the welfare of those affected farmers and because people were not necessarily dependent on bananas for their nutrition.

An African country relying on agriculture might lack such a support system and a bad harvest can have a more detrimental effect, such as famine, on the lives of people in the community. While it would be useful to provide people with what they need at that time, for example replacement crops from other countries, this still would not solve the overall problem. It would make the situation better at that time, but not address the underlying issues of the lack of a safety net to catch people when in need. This calls to mind the analogy to an injury again: individual efforts would provide the plaster to cover up the injury, but they would not help eliminate the cause.

Wolontariat
Voluntary work
POLAND

Sustainability: local action

In order to make a difference on the structural level, a structural approach is needed. And volunteering organisations can provide just that. As already mentioned, they have the expertise and the knowledge of the area to engage people in the 'the right way'. That is, their experience allows them to make a contribution that is feasible and sustainable.

Sustainability has become a commonplace word when talking about development in recent years; sustainability in terms of the longevity of programmes, but also in the approaches that most benefit communities in a cost-effective and efficient way. The maxim of helping people help themselves is the expression of that idea. Volunteering organisations don't aim to make the areas in which they operate dependent on their work, they rather looks at ways in which these areas can achieve long-term sustainable improvement without being forever recipients of external support. One of the main aspects of creating sustainability is the recognition of structures that the global South can offer, rather than imposing a top-down hierarchy from the North. By supporting the development of skills in the South, the future development of those countries can be ensured.

VSO, for example, set up the VSO Federation with overseas organisations to provide development and capacity-building skills in those areas. In the Philippines, VSO has created a partnership with local NGO Bahaginan in Manila. VSO Bahaginan actually started as a pilot programme of VSO International, which is based on a study that was commissioned by VSO in 1998 to try to prove that there are adequate professional skills in the South that can be offered to developing countries. In 1999 they started a five-year pilot programme called the Southern Volunteering Programme, which organised the recruitment of professionals from Kenya and the Philippines and was completed in 2004. After evaluating the results of the achievements of the five-year programme, VSO decided that, based on evidence, there is a pool of professional volunteers from the Philippines and Kenya that can be offered to the global South and that this would potentially change VSO's approach, because previously recruits came only from the North.

As a consequence, since 1998, Bahaginan has expanded from a recruitment base to implementing volunteer programmes. So far, VSO Bahaginan have sent 300 Filipinos overseas to serve as short-term – three to six months – and long-term – two years – volunteers.

In 2003, Bahaginan was registered as a non-governmental development organisation and officially joined the VSO Federation in 2005. In 2010, VSO International will leave the Philippines and pull out of its international volunteering programme, because there will then be adequate social structures and local volunteer-placing organisations. VSO Bahaginan will carry on the work of peace and development independently as an organisation run from the global South and staffed mainly by Southern volunteers.

Zaka
Willing work
PAKISTAN

An important part of sustainability is the ability to recognise community structures in the places of engagement. These can be a great source of support. By involving the local communities directly in projects, the people feel respected and will in return be more likely to commit themselves to work. If skills are shared and implemented in partnership with the providers of volunteering work – the volunteers themselves and the receiving communities – the emerging partnerships can be most fruitful. Robby Nazal, Programme Manager for Volunteering Development and Programme Support at VSO Bahaginan, explained the importance of involving volunteers from the South as well as from the North in their work:

YOUTH STAR CAMBODIA

Youth Star Cambodia is a Cambodian NGO whose aim is to give young people an opportunity to develop their civic leadership skills by working as volunteers in under-served rural areas of Cambodia. Youth Star Cambodia's aim is to build a just and peaceful nation through citizen service, civic leadership, and social entrepreneurship. Their work is guided by the belief that building this is every citizen's right and responsibility, and that each individual can make a difference.

Youth Star volunteers will contribute to rural communities by working in four sectors:

- education and youth development
- sustainable livelihoods
- health and well-being
- business entrepreneurship.

Volunteers with Youth Star Cambodia contribute to all these four areas through a wide range of different activities, such as organising reading programmes or programmes on literacy, the promotion of sustainable livelihoods by training young male and female farmers to increase productivity of their farms using ecologically sustainable and innovative agricultural and animal husbandry practices or by creating young farmers' clubs in order to share information, innovative techniques and good practice.

Youth Star Cambodia volunteers also promote knowledge of hygiene, environmental sanitation, nutrition and common health issues such as malaria, TB, and diarrhoea and iodine and vitamin deficiency through community- and school-based activities and they attempt to engage Cambodia's corporate sector in participating in rural development, particularly to help develop the basic business skills of villagers and to provide market opportunities.

Youth Star's visions for its activities in civic engagement, leadership and social entrepreneurship are that:

- all Cambodian youth will have the opportunity and will want to serve their community and nation
- Cambodian youth will have the values, skills, and inspiration to be leaders for the common good
- Cambodian youth will be catalysts for social transformation and bring creative solutions to the pressing social problems of Cambodia.

Volunteers have been essential to Cambodia's re-emergence from war and destruction. In Year Zero, the year of the end of the Pol Pot genocidal regime, Cambodian men, women and children often returned to their villages to find them destroyed. With little or no outside assistance, people started to rebuild their lives and their communities, often through self-help and the work of local community volunteers. Local *achars*, or Buddhist laymen, mobilised people to rebuild schools and pagodas. Labour co-operatives, or *Krom Samakii*, worked together to put agricultural production back on its feet.

Cambodia has come a long way since then, and Cambodian volunteers are now playing a vital role in reducing poverty and widening horizons in this era of peace and development. Volunteers have set up local self-help groups in their villages, and work with little or no pay to be able to give small loans to poor people to ease them out of debt. They set up local associations that can train villagers to increase their rice yields, or start farming production groups. They train local villagers on laws, and work to resolve conflicts within their communities. Youth volunteers work with their peers to improve their education, encourage them to stay in school and educate them about the dangers of drug use.

Innovative new volunteer programmes have had a strong impact on young Cambodians. Youth Star Cambodia provides one-year service opportunities in under-served rural areas for young Cambodian university graduates. Youth Star's mission is to build a just and peaceful national through citizen service, civic leadership and social entrepreneurship.

Sophea, a Cambodian Muslim woman, applied to Youth Star because she wanted to help develop Cambodia but she needed to learn the necessary skills. She began working in a Cham (Muslim) community. Life was hard at first. Villagers were wary of a young woman who had travelled so far from the protection of her family, and suspected her of being a 'bad' woman with loose morals. But Sophea quickly established trust with the villagers. Soon she started a youth club and arranged for Khmer and English lessons to encourage children who had dropped out of school to return to their studies.

Sophea was also a powerful role model to young women in the village as she encouraged them to further their education and build their futures. As a result, two local girls were accepted to teacher training college. When they return to their villages, their education and confidence will help them make a contribution to developing their communities. In turn, these teachers will be role models for others.

Eva Mysliwiec, Executive Director, Youth Star Cambodia

Youth Star Cambodia
Phnom Penh Centre, Room 132
Corner of Sihanouk (274) and Sothearos (3) Boulevards
Sangkat Tonle Bassac, Khan Chamkar Mon
Phnom Penh (PO Box 171)

Telephone 023-223173–4
Fax 023-223175
E-mail info@youthstarcambodia.org

www.youthstarcambodia.org

'Purely sending international volunteers can be seen as top going down; North going South. We involve volunteers from the South at a community level, and also send Southern volunteers to Africa, South-East Asia, the Balkans, and the Pacific region to support the efforts of developing organisations. This shows that volunteering is not about top-down. It is about bottom-up as well and a matter of appreciating the different values that local *and* international volunteers bring to the whole work of peace and development.'

Sustainability: education

Another source of sustainability in social action is the connection of programmes to education. Education is generally accepted as one of the most important factors of social change. This is why one of the eight UN Millennium Development Goals is to achieve universal primary education by 2015.

Not just doing things for people, but showing them how to do them is the best way to ensure that programmes have a lasting effect within a community. This, some may say, is the sole purpose of education: providing someone with access to knowledge and helping them to attain the means to promote and accomplish change.

The quote by Elbert Hubbert (*right*) can be applied both to development work and volunteering. The aim of the volunteering organisation and the volunteer are to help the receiving individuals or communities support themselves in the future. And the best way of doing this is by sharing experiences and teaching skills with others. The example of VSO Bahaginan is proof of this.

At the same time, education and development work can be directly connected to each other, as a programme run by the University of Witwatersrand (Wits) in Johannesburg, South Africa, shows. The university has set up a Community University Partnerships Unit (CUPS), which enables and promotes civic engagement as an active form of academic citizenship. CUPS provides a home for programmes that bridge academia with society. The Volunteer Programme-Service Learning, is a credit-bearing educational experience in which students participate in an organised service activity that meets identified community need and reflects on service activity in such a way as to gain further knowledge on their course of study. The lecturers develop community-driven projects and students work in the community. Thabo Putu, co-ordinator of CUPS University of the Witwatersrand, explains the concept of service learning:

Gönüllü
Willing work
TURKEY

'The students then come back from working in the community on a project and we then hope that, culturally and academically, they have learned from their experiences. They will grow. They are therefore serving, but they are also learning – the so-called service learning. Both the service and the learning are equal. It is not like an apprenticeship where they train and are concerned about working. The idea is that they work and learn from that. They reflect on their service learning experiences.'

The concept of service learning explained as such reveals an important fact: teaching and learning are not one-way processes, but should rather be developed in a dialectic process between the lecturer, the individual student, and the partner community that they are involved with. When we talked about the qualities that volunteers needed to have, we mentioned openness to new ways of doing things and the willingness to have personal ideas challenged. Service learning is the epitome of such a standpoint.

Then there is a volunteer programme of social responsibility at the university. Wits University Volunteer Programme (WVP) connects the university with the broader community through service, and in so doing shares skill and resources. It also develops a sense of social and

The object of teaching a child is to enable him to get along without a teacher.

ELBERT HUBBARD,
AMERICAN AUTHOR, EDITOR
AND PRINTER

THE UN MILLENNIUM DEVELOPMENT GOALS

In 2000, the UN announced eight Millennium Development Goals, to be achieved by the target date of 2015. These stem from the recognition that in addition to separate responsibilities in individual societies, there is a collective responsibility to ensure principles of human dignity, equality and equity at a global level. More than 30 organisations worldwide, including UNESCO, UNICEF, the World Bank and the Conference of NGOs, work together to attempt to ensure the achievement by 2015. These Millennium Development Goals are:

- eradicate extreme poverty and hunger
- achieve universal primary education
- promote gender equality and empower women
- reduce child mortality
- improve maternal health
- combat HIV and Aids, malaria and other diseases
- ensure environmental sustainability
- develop a global partnership for development.

For more information: www.un.org/millenniumgoals/index.html

Volunteers participate in an HIV and Aids awareness-raising day in Nigeria.

civic responsibility in the university community. Volunteers do all sorts of things, such as teaching, after-school care, running homework centres, and HIV and Aids work. The students at the Wits University Volunteer Programme are involved in about 40 community-based organisations where they are encouraged to give at least two hours of their time each week. In 2007, about 2,000 students were directly involved in various programmes. Although there is no timescale attached to the volunteering, it ranges from three months to a year. However, there are also one-day projects where perhaps up to 500 students work on one major event. Even for those projects, the staff and students at Witwatersrand do a lot of background work.

For instance, in 2007, the Wits University Volunteer Programme organised, together with World Vision South Africa, a march against hunger and poverty. A lot of background work was needed. About 50 students were involved in the preparation and on the day, 200 or 300 students and members of the community participated in the march.

Another event was the Global Youth Service Day, where over 300 students spent a Saturday gardening at and cleaning and painting houses and orphanages. This event was the first of its kind at Wits University and was inspired by similar programmes in 120 countries across the world. Thabo Putu emphasised that although these were one-off events, organised to raise awareness, their students would normally take part in everyday volunteering activities on a more regular basis, to ensure the sustainability of their work.

They also have a lot of fourth- and fifth-year students who are involved in capacity-building for the non-governmental, community-based organisations that are in partnership with the university. Two or three times a week, depending on the level required, the students provide capacity-building by looking at an organisation's strategy and management or its marketing and finance areas. 'The Wits University Volunteer Programme equips student volunteers with leadership and skills through the on-site experiences,' says Thabo Putu.

Global movements and community-based organisations

Other organisations are purely community-based. These involve volunteers mainly from the community they are working in, which allows them greater access to the recipients of voluntary actions. The volunteers who are involved in these organisations are often better placed to make changes and influence in a positive way, as they are not seen as outsiders coming in to 'tell people how to do something', but rather perceived as change agents recruited from their own ranks. With this added credibility, they can push forward agendas of social change.

Often, such organisations are inspired by social movements. Social movements are mainly global phenomena and deal more informally with promoting change than do volunteering organisations or NGOs. They subscribe to a certain agenda, such as climate change, poverty or human rights, and try to influence the general public to be more aware of these issues and, as a consequence, take more action in that field.

Take poverty as an example. Poverty and deprivation are recognised as major global problems, as globalisation has failed to deliver an evenly spread betterment of living conditions around the world. The number one UN Millennium Development Goal is to eradicate extreme poverty and hunger. Fighting poverty has become a massive global movement with supporters worldwide. It finds expression in campaigns that attempt to influence policy-makers, corporations and the public, and encourage them to become more actively involved in helping the disadvantaged.

Swayamsevak
Person
INDIA

SOCIAL MOVEMENT

People with a diffuse sense of collective identity, solidarity, and common purpose that usually leads to collective political behaviour. The concept covers all the different NGOs and networks, plus all their members and all the other individuals who share the common value(s). Thus, the women's movement and the environmental movement are much more than the specific NGOs that provide leadership and focus the desire for social change.

Definition taken from: Baylis, John & Smith, Steve
The Globalisation of World Politics, 3rd ed., Oxford University Press, 2005

Make Poverty History, for example, was an expression of such a global movement. Make Poverty History was a campaign run by a coalition of over 500 British and Irish charities, NGOs, religious groups, campaigning groups and celebrities to raise awareness of extreme poverty around the world and the need to not only address this issue, but also achieve major changes. It was launched in the UK on New Year's Day in 2005. It was the biggest ever anti-poverty campaign and made history with its culmination of activities around the G8 meeting in Gleneagles, Scotland, in 2005. To support the call of 'make poverty history', international artists and bands joined Live 8 concerts that were staged in cities around the globe. White wristbands, the symbol that was chosen to represent the appeal, were worn by people worldwide to show their solidarity with the fight for global social justice. The aim of the campaign was to put pressure on world leaders to make good on their promises to increase and improve aid for the poor, deliver trade justice and provide further debt relief. Make Poverty History and other national campaigns worldwide were part of the Global Call to Action Against Poverty.

волонтерска работа
(Volonterska rabota)

Volunteer work
MACEDONIA

Such a high-profile campaign can help put a social issue on public agendas. The implementation of changed attitudes and perceptions then lies with institutions devoted to the advancement of social change, such as volunteering organisations. They will take the global agenda to their communities, specialise in a specific area and make it relevant for the communities within which they operate. While the campaigns are the advocates of social justice in the world, those organisations are the agents for change.

In Brazil, for example, many organisations have joined the social movement for gender equality. They operate within the communities and try and institutionalise issues of gender equality. These organisations, although being part of a wider global equality campaign, are well-placed to achieve betterment of the gender equality situation in Brazil as they are experts in the culture and social habits of the community. They are thus representatives of a global issue but have specific knowledge of the idiosyncrasies of the communities they deal with.

Take SOS Corpo, for example. The SOS Corpo Feminist Institute for Democracy was founded in 1981 and is located in Recife, north-eastern Brazil. It is a feminist NGO that pursues the democratisation of Brazilian society through the promotion of gender equality and social justice. Such feminist organisations have developed in Brazil as a consequence of its continuing democratisation, but have also played a role in expanding and transforming the traditional notions of democracy and citizenship. It is now considered to be one of the main organisations in the campaign for greater democracy and citizenship in Latin America.

SOS Corpo has developed a strategy of knowledge, education and political action in its fight against poverty, racism and homophobia in Brazilian society, as well as establishing gender equality as an essential aspect of a democratic society. In broader terms, it promotes feminism as a social movement against patriarchal traditions and the dominance of liberal-economic ideology.

Similarly, Casa da Mulher do Nordeste (The House of Women of the Northeast) is a feminist NGO founded in 1980 and is also based in Recife. It campaigns to empower working women and improve their rights and conditions in both private and public spheres and in both private and public production. In particular, it seeks recognition of the women working in family farming, and aims to improve their knowledge of their rights.

Aikin gayya
Collective effort/work
NIGERIA

Social cohesion

In previous chapters, we have talked about the ways in which volunteering can be a tool for social cohesion. Robby Nazal from VSO Bahaginan said that 'the disadvantaged sector can be a part of solving the problem, and not just be the problem'. The concept of involving

---

GENDER EQUALITY IN BRAZIL

In Brazil, many organisations have joined the global movement that is concerned with gender equality. SOS Corpo and Casa da Mulher do Nordeste are two examples of organisations that work within their communities to eradicate discrimination based on gender.

SOS Corpo was founded in 1981 and tries to establish gender equality as an essential aspect of a democratic society by using a strategy of knowledge, education and political action.

www.soscorpo.org.br

Casa da Mulher do Nordeste fights to empower working women and improve their rights and conditions in both the private and public sectors.

www.tdh.org.br/projetos/cmn/index.shtml

socially excluded groups in volunteer work to re-establish their standing in society is not new, and is increasingly applied by volunteering organisations throughout the world. Community Service Volunteers (CSV), the UK's largest volunteering and training organisation, runs several programmes to include volunteers from the social periphery, such as senior citizens or serving prisoners.

For example, they have a particular section of volunteering partners that works specifically with prisons and effects serving prisoners' release for approximately a month to do full-time volunteering. CSV has a 'success rate' of 98 per cent, meaning that in 98 per cent of all volunteer placements, the prisoners complete their jobs and go back to prison without any disruptive incidences. Through the programme, prisoners are sent to partner organisations where they are teamed with local staff, rather than social workers. CSV has a policy of telling only the people directly involved that they are working with a prisoner, in order to break down barriers of social entry. Since the scheme began, CSV has placed more than 3,150 prisoners, who have given more than 500,000 hours to society, often working with some of the most vulnerable people in the community. In an interview with Sue Gwaspari, Volunteering Programme UK Assistant Director at CSV, she commented on the programme:

Shachashabok

Willingly offer services for a noble cause
BANGLADESH

'We team the prisoners with our local staff, but they are just like any other volunteer and we do not tell anyone other than the people who need to know that they are prisoners. But the prisoners do, because they walk straight in on day one and say 'I am a serving prisoner', which is sometimes quite difficult for us because we put them in quite sensitive situations. However, we have developed special opportunities that are safe for them and safe for the people they are working with. Really it is about inclusiveness.'

INVOLVING MARGINALISED GROUPS

Involving marginalised groups in volunteering can be a great agent for social cohesion. Community Service Volunteers (CSV) is the UK's largest volunteering and training charity. It was founded in 1962 and was based on the principle that everyone should be able to take part in the life of their community. The charity runs several programmes that include socially excluded groups in volunteering work for the community. Volunteers for CSV include serving prisoners, the elderly and disabled people.

www.csv.org.uk

Another programme run by CSV is the Retired and Senior Volunteer Programme (RSVP), which looks at ways in which the elderly can be involved in community service. It started as a volunteer programme in 1988 and has now roughly 12,000 volunteers working for them. The idea of a senior volunteer programme grew through the 1960s and 1970s in the USA and was an attempt to harness the skills and expertise of older people for the benefit of local communities, once they had retired from conventional work.

Innovative partnerships

An important aspect of creating sustainable and successful programmes is the issue of partnerships. Many global issues cannot be solved by individual efforts but need to be approached more strategically by a coalition of organisations. The success of Make Poverty History is owing largely to the successful co-operation of so many organisations in shaping the campaign. The University of Witwatersrand stresses partnerships as one of its three pillars of development work, where the university forms partnerships with the government, the community and business.

Kujitolea
Sacrifice; giving one's self
KENYA

Partnerships can also be useful in achieving minority involvement in volunteering. The combination of expertise and knowledge from different organisations can greatly enhance the benefit both for the volunteers and the recipients, because they can advise each other on different issues. While one partner may be very experienced and effective in managing the whole process of volunteer placements in a community, another partner may be familiar with the important structures of that community, while yet another partner may be most aware of the prevailing social concern of a minority.

One such example is a project called Futures, initiated by TimeBank. TimeBank is a British charity and volunteering organisation that was set up to inspire people to volunteer in their communities, and enable charitable organisations and businesses to develop innovative and effective volunteer recruitment programmes. Futures matches people from black and minority ethnic communities with volunteering opportunities to suit their interests and goals. It is run in partnership with Muslim Youth Helpline, a charity that provides faith and culturally sensitive services to Muslim youth especially in the Greater London area, but also in other parts of the UK. Working with the Muslim Youth Helpline ensures that volunteers – mainly Muslims living in the UK – are involved in ways that agree with their personal and cultural backgrounds and social situations, while TimeBank adds the necessary strategic expertise to place volunteers where they are needed, and in a way that benefits both sides. [34]

Time is money?

Time constraints are another major reason why people are reluctant to volunteer. Statistics have shown that the majority of people who are volunteering are either aged 20 or younger, or retired people. One of the main reasons why, in many countries of the global North, people don't volunteer is the lack of time. Due to pressures in the labour market, and the time and effort spent in studying and career development, many people struggle to find time to commit to long-term voluntary projects. Sometimes, the fear of what is to come next in their career paths inhibits any major involvement in social action. Which is why, throughout the world, the concept of flexible volunteering opportunities has been initiated. It provides busy city dwellers with a way of engaging with the community. 'No-commitment volunteering' means that people can volunteer their services for one-off events that usually take place on week nights or weekends. People don't have to sign up for recurring events if they feel they are too busy. This way, barriers of entry are minimised, and the levels of convenience for prospective volunteers are maximised.

GO London, for example, offers a no-commitment volunteering opportunity. Throughout London, regular one-off events are organised on Saturdays and Sundays, lasting about four hours each. The events vary: from painting murals in a community arts centre, helping out at a disadvantaged children's festival, making animal shelters in a city farm, or helping to create a playground jungle in a local school. Each event is attended by 15 to 20 people, and no previous knowledge or existing skills are required. Volunteers sign up for an event, either once or more and, as events take place all over London, they can choose a location

> **Pahinungod**
> Offering oneself
> PHILIPPINES

GO LONDON

GO London offers volunteers flexible, non-commitment volunteering opportunities in the form of one-off events that take place across London on Saturdays and Sundays. They offer busy London professionals a chance of incorporating volunteering into their busy schedules.

www.csv.org.uk/go

HANDS ON MANILA

Hands on Manila is based on an American concept developed in 1992, which offers willing people a chance to volunteer a few hours of their time in a manner that fits their professional and private lives. It is flexible and offers a variety of programmes to choose from.

http://handsonmanila.org.ph

close to their home, to make it even more convenient. These concepts have the advantage of being extremely flexible, which allows them to adapt quickly to any new need that arises in the community.

Similar to GO London, Hands On Manila is a non-profit organisation that provides diverse, flexible volunteer opportunities in central Manila. Established in August 2001, Hands On Manila brings to the Philippines an alternative model of volunteer service, which is flexible enough to allow for volunteering to be integrated into busy, daily schedules. The model was first introduced and developed by the Hands On Network, an alliance of volunteer organisations founded in 1992, and the model has originally been applied in 33 American cities. The flagship project of Hands On Manila is the Hands On Schools-Galing Mo Kid programme. It mentors high-achieving students from lower-income strata with a focus on heroism, environmental awareness and entrepreneurship. Events at Hands On Manila include tutoring, education (computer literacy, health and nutrition), sports and recreation and arts and crafts, among others.

TimeBank also offers volunteering opportunities with very flexible structures to people from all walks of life, by giving volunteers the opportunity to work anything from between an hour a month to a year-long, full-time engagement. It matches the interests and skills of individuals with volunteer opportunities locally, nationally and internationally. It also develops and administers innovative volunteer recruitment programmes and shares best practices to improve the effectiveness of the voluntary sector. Furthermore, TimeBank works with some of the most recognised companies in the UK to plan and promote volunteering. The list of TimeBank's partners includes: public sector partners such as the Cabinet Office, local schools, councils or care centres across the UK; private sector partners such as Starbucks, London 2012 and T-Mobile; and voluntary sector organisations such as the Samaritans and the British Heart Foundation.

Sansana
With good heart
MONGOLIA

TIMEBANK

TimeBank is a British charity that not only looks at finding perfect matches between a volunteer's availability and the community's need, but also looks at the ways in which the voluntary sector can improve its performance. This is partly done through research, but mainly through working in partnerships with other organisations from all three sectors, and allowing the sharing of experiences and best practice from each.

www.timebank.org.uk

PROFILE

The need for co-operation

Many volunteering organisations are now recognising the need for partnerships with other organisations from all three sectors, which we have referred to earlier in the chapter. At this year's annual meeting of the World Economic Forum, world leaders debated on the notion of global citizenship. There was unanimous agreement on the urgent need for major co-operation between public, private and third sectors in order that agents for social change are successful. All three sectors can contribute significantly to the way in which social change is promoted; as many of today's problems are global, these partnerships do not have to be restricted nationally, but can also spread across the world.

Every organisation that manages large volunteer schemes needs to consider strategic issues if they are to succeed in the long term. They will want to step back from the immediate drivers of volunteering – the urgent needs of particular organisations and communities, and the many calls to action from a legion of global problems: disease, malnutrition and human suffering, destitution and displacement visited on the planet by natural disasters and violent conflict. If for a moment they can pause on the brink of filling the critical gaps in skills or labour with the growing number of individuals eager to engage and volunteer, they will need to ask some big questions. One of these is how this individual experience connects with wider networks over space and time to add up to something larger than the personal transformations the experience of volunteering can bring.

We have included in this book many eloquent testimonies to personal change through the experience of volunteering, but they all have something very powerfully in common: the degree of personal insight is directly related to the experience of working in a group. Individual experience is part of a collective experience. Often this is part of working with people in the community who directly benefit from their actions. But very often it is the group of volunteers themselves – living, working and learning together – which is the matrix for this change. The enabling possibilities for these relationships do not occur naturally but are constructed when the scheme is designed and should be regularly reviewed. Here are some of the critical situations:

■ the way volunteers are selected
■ the scope and depth of the induction material
■ the role of the host family
■ the pairing of volunteers
■ the degree of group support, trust and empowerment
■ the way the group interacts among itself and with the community

- the use of translation where needed
- the way the group affiliates with other networks
- the structured learning that takes place
- the way that individuals and organisations plan future action
- the kinds of intercultural skills that are developed and promoted.

In all these areas there needs to be a balance between structure and the creative freedom to evolve. However, it is perhaps in these last two points that the question of design is most significant and where some conceptual tools can be very useful. In the previous chapter we have looked at how the idea of global citizenship can provide the link between an individual action and its wider impact.

For the partners involved in Global Xchange – the British Council and VSO – there is a crucial question as they plan and improve their work: how much can be left to chance to evolve as young people in the scheme meet to effect positive social change? What will lead to a volunteer being more valued in the collective and co-operative mode rather than him or her being viewed simply as an individual whose life has changed? What position leads to this state of affairs and what engagements are critical to the experience and what is her or his destination?

Susu
Mutual help; revolving fund
GHANA

Volunteers discuss global citizenship in Sri Lanka. © Jon Spaull/VSO

GLOBAL XCHANGE

'Today, successful international relations are those where trust is earned by a commitment to mutual understanding, to listening to different points of view, and to accepting that no one country has the monopoly of knowledge and wisdom and that we have much to learn from each other.'
MAKING A WORLD OF DIFFERENCE: CULTURAL RELATIONS IN 2010, BRITISH COUNCIL

'The programme highlighted my belief of how special and diverse people are. Each has his or her own way of seeing, feeling and doing things and this should be respected.'

'I have learned that poverty and inequality affect people's lives in ways far beyond my expectations and that to truly have a valuable impact on sustainable development you must force yourself to think more than you feel. I have learned that despite the diversity that exists in the world there is still more similarities between us than differences. Also that global citizenship and cross-cultural working practices are difficult but achievable, and that peace cannot simply be defined as an end of war, but a state of mind.'

'Global Xchange has been a challenge. It's about volunteering, about living and working with different people, about influencing and changing lives. I guess my Global Xchange experiences have taught me not to over-think things and just make the best out of every situation; it will take small, little steps to change the world.'

'Working across countries and cultures is the only way to dispel the myths we live in, in this so-called age of communication, where miscommunication is more the norm. It widens the horizons of one's worldview and enables it to be reshaped. One never remains the same.'

The Global Xchange partnership

Global Xchange is a six-month international volunteering exchange programme. It is a partnership programme managed and delivered by the British Council, VSO, and a number of local partners around the world. They are committed to the idea that international volunteer exchanges in other activities can develop active global citizens who value volunteering, diversity, community development and social action.

The programme blends the unique contribution of all of the organisations involved to achieve this aim – the British Council, through cultural relations, working with young people, volunteering and programme management expertise; VSO, through international development, programme theme expertise and international volunteering; and the Global Xchange local partners, who bring an understanding of community development and volunteering at the grass-roots level and experience of working with young people through informal education approaches, techniques and methodologies. By working with local partners in this way, the partnership aims to ensure that the programme remains sustainable, works within the appropriate operating contexts and reflects the needs of local people and communities.

The partnership as seen from the perspective of the different partners:

'The approaches we work through to pursue our six development goals at VSO are as important as achieving the goals themselves. In reflecting our values, VSO has identified three main approaches: empowerment, a commitment to learning, and partnership. Through Global Xchange, VSO recognises that our partnership with the British Council and our approach to partnership working within the programme have been integral to Global Xchange's success.

To VSO, the partnership with the British Council to jointly deliver the programme demonstrates and reflects a real commitment to understanding each other's needs; working in a dedicated, equitable and transparent way and working more flexibly to reach our shared vision and objectives. At an operational level a commitment to partnership work continues with our community stakeholders and implementing partners both here and overseas – this inspires all of us at VSO, as Global Xchange exemplifies the way in which the organisation defines good partnership working at every level.'

Marion O'Donnell, Global Xchange Manager, VSO

'Global Xchange directly delivers the British Council's intercultural dialogue agenda by strengthening understanding and levels of trust between people in the UK and other societies, and increasing the ability of individuals and organisations to contribute to positive social change and the strengthening of civil society. The British Council is committed to building partnerships that are reciprocal in nature and which maximise the impact of our work. The Global Xchange partnership between the British Council, VSO and a range of implementing partners and community stakeholders globally is an example of how this has been achieved to the mutual benefit of the partner organisations.

Underpinning our approach to the delivery of the programme is a range of principles and values we have developed as a partnership that encourage mutuality and transparency. This has resulted in an effective partnership, which has provided real opportunities for partner organisations to share experiences and learning, to expand networks and to diversify the delivery of international exchanges that build active citizens, provide tangible benefits to communities, create a greater understanding of how volunteering can effect positive social change, and which contribute to and promote community cohesion globally.'

Tina Murphy, Global Xchange Partnership Director, British Council

'Despite enormous channels of interaction among various nations of the globe and ethnic groups living within countries, stereotypes and misunderstanding persists. This is perhaps due to the way these interactions are constructed both physically and intellectually. A true respect of each other's cultures and values thus remains a distant dream. Global Xchange, in my view, addresses it beautifully. It allows both young men and women of diverse cultures to live with 'alien' host families, work with 'alien' host communities and travel together for six months in each other's countries. This kind of intense and dense interaction can either deepen the existing perceptions or transform the Global Xchange volunteers and host communities.

The first exchange that our organisation hosted in 2005 transformed not only Pakistani volunteers and host communities but also had a lasting impact on the UK volunteers.

Global Xchange volunteers attend a Community Action Day.
© Simon Rawles/VSO

I met some of the UK volunteers in London in January 2007. Every one of them passionately recalled their stay in Pakistan. Each line of their conversation was filled with love and affection for the host families. The members of host families had become host mothers, fathers, brothers or sisters. Their understanding of the roots of poverty, respect of local culture and religion was enhanced. Two examples will suffice to demonstrate the impact of Global Xchange:

The UK volunteers living with poor families, and in an absolutely poor environment, and observing rituals of fasting; and the Pakistani volunteers, sharing a kitchen and dining table, where pork and alcohol might have been served.

As I often visit Global Xchange host communities, I know how much the presence and work of UK volunteers has changed their perception about people in the UK and the West. It has also changed their attitude towards their women, because of the work of women volunteers. Scaling up the Global Xchange model, though a Herculean task, proves that a true interaction can help build a peaceful globe.'

Sarwar Bari, National Co-ordinator, Pattan (implementing partner of Global Xchange)

Global Xchange: vision and aim

Active global citizenship is at the heart of Global Xchange. The programme's vision is to build a world where active global citizens create positive change and build mutual understanding and respect. The aim is 'to develop and inspire global citizens who will create positive change and build mutual understanding and respect between different people'.

Global Xchange defines active global citizens as 'individuals who learn from the experience of others around the world, have an awareness of issues facing all countries, and who put that learning into action'.

Background

Originally based on the Canada World Youth programme, the British Council's Connecting Futures programme and VSO's World Youth Programme, Global Xchange is an exciting and innovative approach to international volunteering by young people.

The programme aims to change positively the lives of individuals and communities through cross-cultural, reciprocal and mutually beneficial international exchanges, and other activities.

Global Xchange operates across the globe but offers dramatic local impact. Volunteers, aged between the ages of 18 and 25 and from all walks of life, can join the programme – providing that they can demonstrate flexibility as well as a commitment to working with others and engaging in experiential and reflective learning. Teams of 18 young people undertake the programme, with equal numbers from the UK and a partner country. The volunteers live and work in the host communities for up to three months in the UK and up to three months in the partner country.

Two programme supervisors, one from the UK and one from the partner country, develop, support and manage each exchange programme. Programme supervisors facilitate the volunteer and community learning for the duration of the exchange. Community stakeholders, volunteer hosts, and programme supervisors have many opportunities during the programme, and as part of the monitoring and evaluation process, to reflect, share, document and learn from their experiences.

Exchanges to date

Since 2005, Global Xchange has delivered 35 individual bilateral exchanges, in 16 countries overseas and over 24 UK communities. These have involved 590 volunteers, 426 host homes, 376 volunteer placements and 54 communities globally. Details of the UK and overseas communities who have participated in the programme to date are:

2005	2006
■ Bandung (Indonesia) – Bristol (England)	■ Malang (Indonesia) – Glasgow (Scotland)
■ Ibadan (Nigeria) – Glasgow (Scotland)	■ Calabar (Nigeria) – Bristol (England)
■ Taldykorgan (Kazakhstan) – Torfaen (Wales)	■ Davao (Philippines) – Bradford (England)
■ Bukhara (Uzbekistan) – Bradford (England)	■ Makassar (Indonesia) – Birmingham (England)
■ Davao (Philippines) – Luton (England)	■ Calabar (Nigeria) – Edinburgh (Scotland)
■ Kupang (Indonesia) – King's Lynn (England)	■ Queenstown (South Africa) – Selby (England)
■ Jos (Nigeria) – Birmingham (England)	■ Tilonia (India) – Gatwick (England)
■ Multan (Pakistan) – Selby (England)	■ Taldykorgan (Kazakhstan) – Hounslow (England)
■ Garhwal (India) – Glasgow (Scotland)	

2007	2008
■ Davao (Philippines) – Southampton (England)	■ Aleppo (Syria) – Glasgow (Scotland)
■ Mombasa (Kenya) – Harlow and Bishop's Stortford (England)	■ Padang (Indonesia) – Harlow and Bishop's Stortford (England)
■ Mzuzu (Malawi) – Caithness (Scotland)	■ Iligan (Philippines) – Newham (England)
■ Sukhbaatar (Mongolia) – Luton (England)	■ Mombasa (Kenya) – Newry (Northern Ireland)
■ Iligan (Philippines) – Bradford (England)	■ Assiut (Egypt) – Luton (England)
■ Rangpur (Bangladesh) – Hounslow (England)	■ Salima (Malawi) – Manchester (England)
■ Lafia (Nigeria) – Brighton (England)	■ Moiplaas (South Africa) – Swansea (Wales)
■ Elmina (Ghana) – Southwark (England)	
■ Kavrepalanchok (Nepal) – Birmingham (England)	
■ Multan (Pakistan) – Truro (England)	
■ Kano (Nigeria) – Rhondda Cynon Taf (Wales)	

Volunteer and community learning

Volunteer and community learning are crucial to the success of any Global Xchange. Through the volunteers' engagement with communities, both volunteers and communities are inspired to learn more about global citizenship and global issues, challenge pre-existing attitudes and values and have opportunities to develop new skills and knowledge.

The programme has developed a Global Citizenship Framework, in partnership with Oxfam, which frames volunteer and community learning to achieve maximum impact. The Framework is based on informal education approaches and methodologies that develop active global citizens and enable volunteers and community members to relate their experiences of Global Xchange to their personal development as global citizens. The Framework focuses on five main areas:

■ poverty and inequality

■ diversity

■ community development

■ volunteering

■ social action.

Within the programme there are multiple opportunities for learning and reflection. Learning baselines are set so the programme can be accredited. These opportunities occur within the core components of the exchange, which are outlined overleaf.

Programme themes

Each exchange has an overarching theme. Examples of themes include HIV and Aids, participation and governance, disability, interfaith, secure livelihoods, youth leadership and peace and development. These themes essentially help shape the volunteer placements and contribute to a recognised need in a host community.

Volunteer placements

Counterpart pairs of volunteers work in local organisations for four days each week for the duration of the exchange. Volunteer placements vary and have included: peer education programmes on educational health projects; programmes working with the elderly and the physically and mentally disabled; educational assistance in schools; and work in marginalised communities such as refugee organisations and asylum seekers.

Example of a volunteer placement from the 2007 Sukhbaatar (Mongolia) and Luton (UK) exchange

Basic and secondary education service

This volunteer placement focused on teacher and classroom support, with the aims of:

- increasing the participation of student/social worker interaction in schools
- organising basic English and computer training among the students
- developing students' oral ability in spoken English
- improving English language knowledge of teachers.

The volunteers worked closely with the teaching staff and students throughout their placement. The impact of their work resulted in the strengthening of the student/social worker relationship and understanding, with many students feeling more comfortable about approaching the social worker. Many of the students developed their English skills rapidly from making the connection with the Global Xchange volunteers, and the teachers furthered their English skills and developed more cultural understanding of the UK, helping to put more context into their lessons.

Community Action Days

The Community Action Days are an opportunity for an entire exchange team to get together each week to work on a big project or task where many pairs of hands are needed. Teams are often approached by local organisations to participate in an activity that addresses a particular community need. Past examples of such initiatives have included cultural and global education days for local schools, community clean-ups, development awareness days, and fund-raising events for local charities and causes.

Example of a Community Action Day
from the 2006 Calabar (Nigeria) and Edinburgh (UK) exchange

The aim of this Community Action Day (CAD) was to gain an understanding of what it is like to be orphaned and to learn about the establishment in which the orphans reside. The team spent the day at a Nigerian orphanage to gain an understanding of what 'a day in the life' looked and felt like for the occupants.

The volunteers interacted with the young orphans and the abandoned old people by talking and sharing their experiences of Nigeria and the UK. They played games with the young orphans as well as offering company to and assisting with the chores for the elderly. The latter involved carrying out maintenance and cleaning responsibilities.

The volunteers experienced what a typical Saturday is like in a Nigerian orphanage/old people's home. The residents had a chance to meet people from different cultures, exchanging stories, experiences and learning. The end result was that awareness was raised about the issues faced by orphans and abandoned elderly people.

Global Citizenship Days

Each week during the exchange, all 18 volunteers come together as a team for a Global Citizenship Day. Throughout the six-month programme, each volunteer manages two Global Citizenship Days. These provide an opportunity for the volunteers to engage in active learning about community development issues in the UK and in the exchange country. These are organised by the volunteers and focus on a topic relating to global citizenship. Examples of Global Citizenship Days have included those focusing on fair trade, education, climate change, and debt.

**Example of a Global Citizenship Day
from the 2006 Taldykorgan (Kazakhstan) and Hounslow (UK) exchange**

Learning objectives:

- defining homosexuality

- discuss laws relating to homosexuality

- discuss problems that gay, lesbians and bisexuals face, such as discrimination, religion and HIV and Aids

- discuss social action taken to reduce discrimination (gay pride events).

The group worked through the objectives and discussed them in the context of the UK, Kazakhstan and the international community, focusing particularly on discrimination, and its effects (short- and long-term) on the individual and the community.

Religious attitudes were also discussed and a psychologist from the local university was invited to speak to the group to explain the negative reaction to homosexuality and how to prevent it from causing harm.

At the end of the Global Citizenship Day the volunteers had thought about and discussed many major issues faced by those discriminated against for homosexuality, breaking down any negative preconceptions held while supporting positive perceptions within the group.

Challenges

For participants of Global Xchange, knowledge, learning and experience is derived from direct personal engagement and developed through structured reflection, which helps people contemplate themselves, the team, the work and wider issues. Of course, a volunteering experience will not always run smoothly. Global Xchange has seen conflict and frustration as a result of the very challenging environment that volunteers find themselves in.

Living and working with a counterpart from another country is a challenge that most volunteers we interviewed referred to. Volunteers move from not knowing their counterparts to spending most of their time with them – and this can lead to interpersonal conflict. All volunteers, as they work in communities that are not their own, are required to leave their comfort zone, with all their social networks, behind them and immerse themselves in the new.

This is important, as it allows volunteers to consider their own cultural background more closely; they are given the opportunity to look at their own culture from an outsider's perspective. This helps in making them more critical and reflective about the things that go on in their own homes. Besides raising cultural awareness and intercultural competencies, this also contributes to the development of conflict management and resolution.

This is further advanced by the fact that volunteers on the programme are part of a team. It increases the challenge of considering one's own personal opinions and overcoming obstacles and requires the volunteers to engage on a wider level. The challenge is increased by the fact that Global Xchange teams represent a cross-section of both countries that are represented, incorporating diversity in terms of geography, gender and ethnicity.

The volunteers are encouraged to speak their mind and share their thoughts on the progress they feel that they are achieving. This has prompted Mark Vrionides, one of the Global Xchange volunteers,

Maija Paasiaro, a volunteer working with the Mongolian farmers' association in Ulaan Baatar, teaching English to members of the association. Maija is also working to increase their access to funding. © Jon Spaull/VSO

to deliver a speech to his team and supervisors at one of the Global Citizenship Days of his programme, in which he stresses the importance of dialogue and negotiation for the advancement of learning and team building:

'I am learning a lot about myself, about my skills, my needs for development, and about my often unconscious effect on others, but I am doing this individually, not collectively. This has led to tensions that no one is addressing openly. And I feel that these, avoided and not properly dealt with, are dissuading people from truly committing to team efforts and hindering our sense of focus.

Somewhere within this active global citizen, Buddhism and Global Xchange have quite unexpectedly collided. There is a strong Buddhist belief that any strong negative reactions to other people or their behaviours come from within the person who is reacting. This is summed up in the saying that 'it is your mind that creates this world'. In other words, when you feel angry about something or someone, that anger is created by you or your mind, not by the something or someone. I have used anger as an example; the belief equally applies to any human emotion or perception. However, this belief can lead to false sensations of guilt or responsibility for such reactions. Occasionally over the past few months, this is how I have been feeling. Global Xchange has brought such feelings to my head and prompted considerable self-reflection.

As an experience in team-building, Global Xchange so far seems like a failure. In terms of work placement achievements, familial and community assimilation and counterpart bonding, everything is going very well. But as far as the team is concerned, we're not getting very far. I am learning a lot about myself, about my skills, my needs for development, and about my often unconscious effect on others, but I am doing this individually, not collectively. This has led to tensions that no one is addressing openly. And I feel that these, avoided and not properly dealt with, are dissuading people from truly committing to team efforts and hindering our sense of focus.

As for me, my own contribution to this team's shortcoming and lack of development is this misunderstood sense of Buddhist guilt, coupled with a general characteristic passivity. Both of these have encouraged an avoidance of conflict.

A Community Action Day, the volunteers working on the garden at the Camilla School for Children with Learning Difficulties, in Colombo, Sri Lanka.

© Jon Spaull/VSO

I am keen to break free. I have achieved this through reflection on myself and on my beliefs. Not for the first time in my life have I found great wisdom in Gautama Buddha's doctrine of no-self or *anatman*. In this doctrine, Buddha defined all aspects of what we see as the Self, including our perceptions, emotions and even our physical forms as uncontrollable, temporary and a source of suffering. This led Buddha to rephrase 'it is your mind that creates this world, including the idea that mind is yours'. Such clarity helps one accept everything that the mind has to offer with patience, an absence of guilt, and even a sense of expectancy. I am now ready to face conflict and tension with clarity, politeness and realism. In conflict resolution, compromise is more about meeting your 'dissenters' head on, and working together to find a middle ground that satisfactorily incorporates something of both sides' wishes, rather than giving up on one's own wishes or opinions. It is unrealistic to assume that we all have to get on just fine, smooth as silk, and as the best of intercultural friends for us to best represent active global citizens. I am not asking for us to create conflict, but please let's not ignore it, hide or wait it out when it comes. We'll learn much more from doing exactly the opposite.

I am looking forward to my next moment of anger.'

Mark Vrionides, Global Xchange volunteer, Edinburgh, UK, with Calabar, Nigeria
September 2006 to March 2007

The programme has the biggest impact on the young people who volunteer, but its power extends to the families who host them, the community projects with which they work and the wider communities in which they live. The fact of working so closely with a counterpart and the team helps to promote the awareness of others and raise sensitivity towards fellow human beings. As part of a pair, or a team, the volunteers cannot be selfish and stubborn but need to re-evaluate their position and attitude on a constant basis. This is supported by the fact that volunteers are so strongly encouraged to engage in self-reflection.

In this way, Global Xchange demonstrates the potential, and promotes the values of active global citizenship for all the participants. The idea is that volunteers can learn a great deal about another country and culture through talking, working and living with someone from that country. They can also support each other through the experience – the UK volunteer will support their overseas counterpart during the UK phase and vice versa. They can act as cultural guides, practice language with each other, and show each other the delights and features of their own countries.

'I was on the programme between Malang, Indonesia, and Glasgow, UK. We started out in Indonesia on our first phase, and while I was there my work placement was in a school for the blind – it was the only one on the whole of Java. It was amazing. Before we went we certainly did not know what to expect, and we had heard some really awful things about disability, which was the theme of our exchange, and how people with disability are treated there. I was really nervous, but when we went to the school it was great. The students were so positive and enthusiastic about having us there and the things that we could do. Our exchange partners were the scouts, and we ended up setting up the scout movement in the school because they said they did not have any sort of extracurricular activities. Scouts are very popular in Indonesia, and a lot of that can come into the things that scouts do. They also wanted to learn English; as soon as they learned they had two English volunteers, they asked if they could have English lessons, which was something really easy that we could do that they were really positive about. It was amazing because they have a disability, but they are so incredibly positive about everything. That was probably what I learned most: a positive attitude can get you so, so much, and they probably taught me more than I ever gave back to them.

We were living in host homes out there, which was a big learning experience. I had never been to Asia, and it was really interesting to live in a predominantly Muslim country, which is something that has interested me, but I do not really know much about any of the world's religions apart from Christianity, which I am quite familiar with. It was really interesting from that point of view to be in such a religious country and seeing that first hand. There were lots of interesting new experiences out there.

One of the reasons I wanted to do Global Xchange was that you get to be in the UK, as well, and the Indonesians come back with you. It was fascinating to come back to Glasgow and hold a mirror up to your own culture and really see it for what it is, with all the things you take for granted. Suddenly you have someone else saying: 'Why do you do this?' You have a real chance to think about what is good about how the UK is and what is good about how other countries are, and what you can take away from each to think about how you would want a country to develop in a good and positive way. I think the Indonesians were quite shocked at how deprived some areas of Glasgow were because they had expectations that it would just be like what you see in Hollywood movies, and it really is not. I think they were shocked about how much they could bring by volunteering and how much difference they could make in a country where they thought there would not be anything they could improve and that it would all be them learning what is good. I think it gives you, on both sides, a new appreciation of some things in your own country and a real kind of shock about other things. That definitely worked both ways, which was really interesting. Our work placement was with the Scottish Interfaith Council, so it was really interesting to learn about multiculturalism and interfaith work. That was something that I had never been at all involved in before. I still keep in touch with my work placement; I have gone up and done youth workshops with them since then and stayed involved, which has been really nice.'

Daisy Streatfeild, Global Xchange volunteer, Malang, Indonesia, with Glasgow, Scotland March to September 2006

VOLUNTEERING: BENEFITS FOR THE UK

The UK is an extraordinarily wealthy country by global standards, being in the G8 group of nations that shares 44 per cent of the world's gross domestic product compared with the nine per cent shared by Africa and Latin America combined.[35] Indeed, the G8 represents approximately 14 per cent of the world population, but they account for 65 per cent of the world's GDP.[36] So the UK would seem to be a society almost entirely at the supply side of volunteering, sending many volunteers to developing nations each year. For example, VSO alone has almost 1,500 skilled professionals working throughout the developing world.

And yet, there are problems besetting parts of UK society that derive from its very economic success and these problems are very susceptible to help from international volunteers. This section looks at some of these problems and how international volunteering is starting a trend that could find solutions. For our example, we look at Luton, a medium-sized town in the south-east of England in the UK and at the impact that Global Xchange has on the community through the viewpoint of just one of numerous community organisations in that city.

The numbers: shares of world GDP: [37]	1820	1975	2004
G8	29%	55%*	44%
(USA only)	2%	22%	21%
China	33%	5%	13%
India	16%	3%	6%
Latin America	2%	7%	6%
Africa	5%	3%	3%

*50% without Russia, about 55% with

So what are the kinds of problems experienced by the UK as part of its success? The industrial revolution started the process whereby the countryside was depopulated as workers deserted agriculture to seek their livelihoods in urban industries. The unplanned growth of cities is a global phenomenon of course,[38] but the infrastructures of certain cities struggle to provide services to their citizens, or ensure equality of access to health, housing, education, access to leisure and creative pursuits. The results are deprivation, poverty, crime and social disintegration. The rapid economic progress stimulated by the monetarist policies of the Conservative governments (1979–97) have come with a price. There is no such thing as society, said Margaret Thatcher (British Prime Minister, 1979–90), and there has been a progressive disintegration of the traditional institutions that bind societies together in the decades since.

One of the positive legacies of the UK's Empire has been multiculturalism and the openness that this brings. There is a special dynamism that one can feel in living, eating, shopping, experiencing the arts, worshiping or being educated in contemporary UK cities. However, it also raises special issues for community relations. The UK trend has not been one where new immigrants have subordinated their identities and *assimilated*. In fact, the most successful communities are ones where some pattern of integration has succeeded and a new kind of creative forging of civic relationships has occurred; individual cultural traditions flourish but there is an overall sense of an overarching identity as a citizen with rights and responsibilities to all. But there is always a tension, sometimes a creative one, sometimes not, which means that solutions to problems are constantly being negotiated. Communication and understanding between groups and communities can be especially fragile and disrupted by events. These can be local or international.

Often tensions between ethnic and religious minorities have led to divides not just within affected communities but also those far away. The aftermath of 9/11 and the transport bombings in Madrid and London, have seemed to license a worldwide Islamophobic backlash. When, in 2006, cartoons mocking the Prophet Muhammad were printed in Danish newspapers, demonstrations and riots protesting about these cartoons swept across the globe. Although these events resonate with mass audiences, it is in local communities where they are felt most sharply. It is in everyday life that the consequences of such tensions manifest themselves most dramatically, leading to polarisation and then, through progressive stages of disillusion, to alienation, social exclusion and deprivation.

Local community organisations (voluntary and community organisations, charities, social enterprises, co-operatives and housing associations) are in the front line, helping to prevent or to mitigate the problems raised by deprivation, social exclusion or by cultural miscommunication. They tackle a wide range of issues. Below we look at how one organisation, Grassroots, in Luton, benefits not just from volunteering but from international volunteering and the concept of global citizenship.

What sort of town is Luton? The nickname of the local football team, The Hatters, gives a clue to the city's industrial past in hat-making, just one of many light manufacturing industries to be carried on there. The same straw that made hats, also made bricks. These industries wax and wane, bringing jobs and prosperity at their height and then bringing their opposites as they decline. It is a constant process of ebb and flow, which comes with a social cost each time. The trend, as in much of the UK is for manual industry to be replaced by service industries. In Luton, brick-making and car manufacture have gone, to be replaced in part by jobs in the expanding Luton airport nearby.

The promise of jobs has also attracted waves of incomers from other parts of the world. Italians came first to work in the brick-making industry, followed by Irish people, who were attracted by the building of the motorway. They have been followed by people from Africa, the Caribbean and South Asia. The present composition of the population of 184,371 according to the 2001 Census looks like this:

Christian	59.65%	British White	64.97%
Muslim	14.62%	Pakistani	9.23%
No religion	14.08%	Irish	4.65%
Religion not stated	7.23%	Caribbean	4.15%
Hindu	2.73%	Bangladeshi	4.14%
Sikh	0.81%	Indian	4.09%
Other religions	0.35%	Mixed – White/Black	2.56%
Jewish	0.29%	Other White	2.28%
Buddhist	0.25%	African	1.74%
Chinese and other ethnic	0.93%	Other Asian	0.81%
Other Black	0.45%		

So there is a complex interaction of economic, ethnic and cultural changes that shape Luton's identity as a multifaith and multicultural community. These factors enrich and energise the community at the same time as they inform its tensions and conflicts.

Grassroots, an interfaith charity, works in one of the town's areas of deprivation – places that have levels of unemployment and exclusion that stand in stark contrast to the prosperous south-east of the UK. The challenge is regeneration and renewal, especially in Luton's peripheral housing estates. Grassroots plays a role in meeting this challenge, a role that David Jonathan – 'Johny' – says is greatly helped by international volunteering. For one thing internationalism is at the heart of what Grassroots, and he personally, are trying to do there. Having come to the UK from north-west India six years ago, where he worked for the YMCA, he wondered just how aware such a powerful G8 nation could become about the world beyond it and how clearly it could see the darker side of the process of globalisation. However, he found the fabric of the UK's multicultural society, composed by so many diasporic groups, had an inbuilt awareness of international issues. Living in India, the issue of Kashmir was never as vivid as it was when discussed by émigré groups in Luton.

Global Xchange has brought him a series of not only British but also international volunteers, who have enhanced the objectives of his organisation in powerful and subtle ways. Where particular ethnic groups have tended to keep their cultures 'preserved in a box', the arrival of a volunteer living in the home country can provide a different, updating perspective, which challenges that static picture. However, it doesn't need to be a visitor from the same country to provoke reflection. He recalls the impact on Luton's Pakistani Muslims on seeing women volunteers from the Philippines playing football.

One of his objectives is to increase interfaith understanding so that the spirituality and wisdom of different faiths be shared more effectively. Many citizens of Luton do not have a faith, so the role of activists from different faith-based organisations is to work together for the benefit of the community by exercising their goodwill. The presence of young international volunteers allows Grassroots to increase its reach and reputation by gaining the trust of a wider range of the population. They make the host families aware of the activities of the organisation and they also bring their passion for justice and the ideals of global citizenship.

Global citizenship is another objective of Johny's work. He shares the questions volunteers also ask themselves: How do we use the benefits of globalisation to build a world that is sustainable, creative, peaceful and just? How do we develop a world view that is not Eurocentric and is able to accommodate the perspectives of people from the South and East? How do we challenge those forces that are concerned only with their personal wealth and security at the expense of the death and suffering of others? Their enthusiasm contributes to the campaign to make Luton a fair trade town and their critique of an excessively materialistic approach to life, exemplified by their personal conduct in volunteering, is in harmony with European organisations such as Kairos Europa, which echoes Grassroots's spiritual approach. [39]

Because the volunteers are paired together in placements, one from the UK and one from the other country in the exchange, there is a very special dynamic as they learn from each other, compare countries and cultures and reflect on their experience at Grassroots and other organisations in the town. The volunteers meet to run Global Citizenship Days.

Global Citizenship Days have been held on a range of themes – youth development and training; health development; understanding volunteering; volunteering in different countries and communities; refugees and asylum seekers; and communism and democracy. Events have also been held on cultural traditions, such as the Mongolian Festival celebrating Nadam, and there has also been a mobile travelling presentation on fair trade.

Young people volunteering in Luton have been involved in exchanges with the Philippines, Mongolia and Egypt. We spoke to some who came from Mongolia and asked them about how they viewed poverty in the UK. For them, in one sense, it did not exist, because they always saw a 'safety net' of welfare, which could be absent in other parts of the world, including their own sometimes. But they were clear that there was deprivation and there was inequality, which they were helping to change.

Johny rates the value of social capital as paramount, including the values of the faith communities he brings together. However, he avoids the expression 'building social capital' – he sees it as being 'uncovered' rather than built. It is there to be discovered and realised, with the help of Global Xchange and other volunteers who come to work with him and his three colleagues.

Endnotes

33   Salamon, L. M., Sokolowski, S. W. & Associates (2004) *Global Civil Society: Dimensions of the Nonprofit Sector,* vol. 11, Bloomfield, CT: Kumarian Press

34   http://futuresproject.org.uk
www.myh.org.uk
www.timebank.org.uk

35   Progressive Policy Institute: www.ppionline.org/ppi_ci.cfm?knlgAreaID=108&subsecID=900003&contentID=253413

36   Source: International Monetary Fund, *World Economic Outlook Database*, October 2007

37   Ibid.

38   See Mike Davis' book *Planet of Slums* and his arguments about super slums, Verso Books, 2006

39   www.kairoseuropa.de/fix/english.html

CHAPTER 4

GLOBAL CITIZENS

'Global citizenship goes beyond knowing that we are citizens of the globe; it is a way of thinking and behaving. It is an outlook on life – a belief that we can make a difference and make the world a better place. Young people are growing up in an increasingly global context. Many will live, work and study alongside people from all over the world. More and more people are travelling for work or for leisure. All forms of culture are shaped by global influences. Each decision we make as professionals, consumers or voters has an impact on global society.'

INSTITUTE OF INTERNATIONAL EDUCATION, HONG KONG

An Education Activity Day in Sri Lanka: volunteers visiting a herb garden where the local hospital sources the ingredients for its traditional Ayurvedic medicines. © Jon Spaull/VSO

GLOBAL CITIZENS

As we have seen from the previous chapters, volunteering can be a very powerful tool in achieving social change. The ways in which just one volunteer can make a positive contribution is reflected in the stories of those involved. Volunteering can also be a way of being a global citizen in the world.

In times where people across the world are increasingly interconnected and the challenges of the world tend to be of global, rather than of local or national scale, volunteering needs to be

> *Claca*
> Mutual support
> ROMANIA

VOLUNTEERING AND GLOBAL CITIZENSHIP

The following quotes were some of the responses we received from Global Xchange volunteers relating to volunteering and global citizenship:

'As a volunteer you have a power that can bring positive change to the community and during volunteering you can develop yourself and gain lots of skills as well; if other people realised these things, I think, they could not be not interested in volunteering.'

'Volunteers certainly gained the skills very clearly in terms of event management, community work, community mobilisation and discovering complexities and sensitivities of community work, particularly when it happens across faiths, cultures and nationalities.'

'Others may plant the roots, some might water the plant. The plant may take some time to grow. But it will, given proper care and patience. And then you'll know that you have made a change and a difference.'

'I now see myself as a person that can make a difference and a very big impact on the society even if I have to face challenges.'

'Having never been exposed to community development I can see that in order to try and make a difference you need to be proactive – try to get as many people as possible involved.'

'Volunteering made me realise that my country and my community need people like us volunteers, who will help and play a very vital role in development and progress.'

'Volunteering is such a powerful tool for social action since it tries to spread positive influence to other people and sends a message that "yes we can do it if we do it together".'

'Community development is a long process since it is not a one-shot goal. Global citizenship does not mean being able to travel, rather it aims to bind people and culture from different parts of the world, a message that says "we are global citizens, therefore it is our responsibility to care for others especially those who are deprived in this world".'

'Volunteering is involving yourself in what is happening in your community and playing a role to resolve any conflicts and searching for excellence and development of the community.'

'Social action is making a difference and making a change – not just accepting things as they are.'

'We don't see things the way they are, we see things the way we are.'

THINK GLOBAL, ACT LOCAL

'The challenges of our age are global; they transcend national frontiers; they are problems without passports. To address them, we need blueprints without borders. That is why, more than ever before, we need dedicated and talented young men and women to be global citizens who make the choice of service to humankind.'
KOFI ANNAN

As a consequence of globalisation, problems have moved to a truly global scale. Volunteering can help us be aware of this global interconnectedness, but as a part of this, it also needs to be increasingly global in its outlook as issues transcend national boundaries. Kofi Annan's quote is so resonant in its ways of describing the importance of thinking global we have quoted it again.

The one facet of globalisation that is completely beyond dispute is the fact that communication technology has massively increased global communication; a small group in Chapas in Mexico, fighting for indigenous rights for example, can communicate with a small group in Manchester that is trying to increase community cohesion. There are links that are made and shared, in turn. There is an increased sense of people all over the world in some ways having similar concerns and often fighting the same battles and finding the ways they can work together.

Having a global perspective is important, as it can help us put our own community or society in relation to other places around the world. On the one hand, this can be quite a depressing experience. Actually seeing a famine in Ethiopia or floods in Bangladesh is quite different to hearing about them on the news. But although this will necessarily be quite humbling, it can also put our own society and problems in relation to where they sit in the world. It makes us aware of those issues that affect us as well, not just people overseas. Witnessing extreme poverty or social injustice somewhere else, can lead to us being quite alienated upon our return home. All of a sudden, those parts of our daily lives that were natural to us, are put into question. Fresh water, which was taken for granted, becomes a commodity to appreciate and handle with respect. Having a truly global perspective on those problems that affect humanity, can be an eye-opener to the things we consider important and those that need to be prioritised.

With this broadened world view, we can also address issues that affect people in their own communities. Poverty or human rights abuses are not restricted to certain parts of the world – they manifest themselves in almost every society in the world, although they may take different forms and guises. We can take our learning from other parts of the globe and put it into action in our everyday lives, not just overseas. As we increasingly realise that all societies in the globe are bound by one common thread – our humanity – we can strive to share not only good practice between societies, but also our diverse knowledge, so that we eventually reach some kind of universal knowledge that benefits all of mankind.

Thinking global is also useful when looking at international conflicts, based on ethnicity, politics, resources, religion or other interrelated areas. By engaging in cross-cultural experiences, we look at another society's everyday life, rather than just getting a fairly superficial tourist experience. We share different aspects of our culture and establish intercultural relationships. This is not only attractive to young volunteers, it also supports resolving international conflicts through channels of intercultural dialogue. By understanding the diversity in which we live, and also the commonalities between different societies, we are better placed to make a lasting positive contribution to social change, both locally and therefore globally.

reassessed in this new framework. As much as globalisation is a hotly debated issue, global citizenship is much discussed by governments, organisations and populations everywhere in the world. At the same time, the recognition that the problems we are facing are increasingly global and the desire to achieve global social justice and equality adds significance to this debate and stresses the urgency of addressing global responsibilities, accountability and governance.

Cosmopolitanism

The idea of human beings existing not solely as individuals but as part of a wider community is not new. As we have seen in Chapter 2, Diogenes already called himself a 'citizen of the world' in his lifetime, roughly 2,400 years ago. This idea of cosmopolitanism refers to the perception that all of humanity is connected and opposes the idea that we are merely part of independent communities or states. As human beings, we have moral obligations to all fellow human beings, not merely those from our own community or our fellow citizens. Throughout the 20th century, the nationalist movements of the previous centuries were counteracted by an exponential rise in modern transport systems, and information and communication technologies across borders. But cosmopolitanism is more than internationalism. It is not merely about the ways in which we interact with people from other countries and cultures, it is how we actively contribute to their lives and how they are affected by our actions and behaviour.

> *Bulungi bwensi*
> Good of the kingdom
> UGANDA

Global citizenship forms part of this debate on cross-cultural responsibilities, accountabilities and obligations. Global citizenship as a term refers to being caught up in a global web of interconnectedness with other parts of the world, in which people on one side cannot ignore the problems of people on the other side, in which social justice and equality need to be addressed by us all, rather than a few, in order to overcome some of the difficulties that the world faces. Global citizenship is the acknowledgement that we cannot solve most of the world's humanitarian problems within the boundaries of our nation states or communities, but that we all need to pull together in order to reach global social betterment.

Towards a definition: global citizenship and volunteering

One of the questions we asked volunteers in our interviews for this publication was: 'What does global citizenship mean to you?' Although the answers were quite varied, a few common threads ran through all replies. Global citizens have an awareness and understanding of the issues that have an impact not just in their own community, but also those that affect people globally. Through volunteering, many of them learned that they were bound to other people through their commonalities, rather than set apart by differences. Volunteering for them was a way of participating in another community and seeing how social change is tackled in other parts of the world. This often led to the questioning of their societies, the experience having enlightened them about the problems that people across the world face, but also to those issues that work well at home. Some said that they recognised that all over the planet, people are fighting for the same humanitarian issues, whether they call it social or community cohesion or the right to participate in their own societies. This can help increase intercultural respect and understanding. It can help us in becoming, what one volunteer called 'world wise'.

Nyanja
To help
ZAMBIA

ASPECTS OF COSMOPOLITANISM

Being 'cosmopolitan' used to mean no more than a complimentary description of an enlightened citizen of the world – learned and cultivated individuals whose often elite lifestyles encompassed the cultures of the world, whether they travelled between 'civilizations', across empires, or simply made a major capital city, where cultures meet, their home. Now, with a more globalised world, this word creates debate when it is used. It is a discussion about political ethics – the right and wrong of social action, which starts with religious thinkers and philosophers but has some very practical implications, especially for volunteering and global citizenship.

There was increasing internationalism at the end of the 19th and 20th centuries. In 1893, the World's Parliament of Religions met in Chicago for the first time, the United Nations was founded in 1945 and, in 1948, the Universal Declaration of Human Rights was formulated. However, national interests and agendas now increasingly control multilateral institutions and neither a world government nor a world religious leadership has gained any major ground.

The world we glimpse in this new era of internet and telephony communication, hyper-travel and global markets, is not one where cultural differences have been diminished, but, rather, have been made more visible. Transparent boundaries replace the border fences of ignorance. We know more about other cultures and as a result we can learn more about who we are as *Homo sapiens*, wherever we live. For the first time, perhaps, we can also realistically consider universal systems that could be applied globally without violation and insensitivity: ecumenical, humanistic, ethical and legal principles applied to policy; and genuinely international political leadership and enforcement brought to bear on global issues such as security, climate, rights, health and a huge range of inequalities. The question for cosmopolitanism is who can become a global citizen. Can cosmopolitanism be only a privileged perspective, and what are the individual duties of these pioneering citizens, what new communities should be formed and what new politics and systems of governance are appropriate? The answers to these questions are as likely to be answered by global citizens as they are by philosophers and religious thinkers. [40]

Many volunteers feel a form of empowerment through the experience. They see that they could share their own knowledge and skills with people from across the globe, but also take back what they have learned to their home communities. Through committing themselves to a wider community, and contributing to the people's and planet's well-being, they feel less awed by the challenges the world faces today. Making a difference, no matter how small, helps them to be more optimistic about achieving positive social change for the future.

The American anthropologist Margaret Mead once said: 'Never doubt that a small group of thoughtful, committed citizens can change the world. Indeed, it is the only thing that ever has.' This recognition is a change that people have felt through volunteering. As they recognise the difference they can make to other people's lives far away from home, global citizens realise that they can't dissociate themselves from the wider community.

Volunteers who are aspiring to be global citizens get their inspiration for action from global issues; but their actions affect first and foremost local communities. They think global, and act local.

Citizenship in a global context?

But surely, if global citizenship is to have significance beyond pure moral obligation and activism, then we need to be clear about the meaning of 'citizenship' in a global context. One of the many reservations people have with the term 'global citizenship' is the word 'citizenship' being used in conjuction with the word 'global'. Should the understanding of citizenship in state terms be identical to that of citizenship on a global scale? Citizenship in the state implies a formal relationship with the state.

Ehrenamtliche Arbeit
Honour work; work for free
GERMANY

Programme supervisors Hannah and Yemi working together on a UK–Nigeria Global Xchange.

GLOBAL CITIZENSHIP FRAMEWORK

The British Council and VSO have, together with Oxfam and past volunteers of the Global Xchange project, created a Global Citizenship Framework, to help the volunteers understand the bigger picture of their involvement. Volunteering can be an important catalyst in understanding global citizenship and our role as global citizens.

Active global citizenship is central to Global Xchange, and it is part of this programme's aim to develop and inspire global young people to become engaged and create positive change as well as build mutual understanding and respect between different people.

As we have mentioned before, the Global Xchange definition of global citizenship is 'individuals who learn from the experience of others around the world, have an awareness of issues facing all countries, and who put that learning into action'.

The Global Citizenship Framework identifies five main areas in global citizenship, which are the focus of Global Xchange:

- poverty and inequality
- diversity
- community development
- volunteering
- social action.

During their six months on the programme, volunteers will learn and reflect on these five topics. Ideally a volunteer will have gained important insights into these five topics.

Poverty and inequality

Throughout the programme, volunteers will see, research, learn and experience poverty and inequality and their causes. Volunteers will look at questions of what they see as poverty and how it is measured. They will research the causes of poverty and inequality and the ways in which these are consequences of past events. They will look at the role of globalisation in this context and learn about the power relationships in addressing and reducing inequality and poverty.

> 'It may come in different forms but the way I see it, poverty is relative. It is inequality that makes people poorer.'

> 'I have learned that there is no poverty if there are no greedy people in the world. There is no inequality if everyone is sharing what he or she has, not matter how big or small. There will be community development if there is collective help.'

Diversity

When exploring diversity, the volunteers will, by living with a counterpart from another country and volunteering in both their home country as well as their counterpart's, learn how people live with difference and how respective societies perceive difference. They will look at issues of identity formation, gender and sexual orientation as well as religion and belief systems, socio-economic status, ethnicity and race, prejudice and discrimination and lifestyle in general.

'The programme highlighted my belief of how special and diverse people are. Each has his or her own way of seeing, feeling and doing things and this should be respected.'

'The world is blessed with unique and talented individuals. As humans, we need to value such uniqueness and respect it.'

Community development

Volunteers on the programme will look at the ways different communities work, how they change and who controls this change. Besides broad questions of understanding what a community is, they will look at issues of sustainability, social inclusion, community cohesion and participation.

'Having never been exposed to community development I can see that in order to try and make a difference you need to be proactive and try to get as many people as possible involved.'

'Community development is an essential factor in the fight to overcome global poverty and individual action can make a real difference practically.'

Volunteering

Volunteers are also actively encouraged to explore why certain people volunteer and how to get involved. Through the cross-cultural exchange, they are exposed to different ideas of volunteering from around the globe and ask questions about the quality of volunteering and the benefits it brings both to the volunteer and the community. Volunteers will also look at the voluntary sector and its impact overall and what it does.

'By doing little things and starting it right, we can create an impact in slowly changing the lives of people for the better.'

'I think this experience really shows how much of an impact/difference just a few people sharing their skills can make.'

Social action

As a last point, volunteers will look at how to increase motivation and the ability to bring about change and the belief that we can all contribute. The personal experience they have will allow them to experiment with and test different methods of involvement in social action. These topics include advocacy, social responsibility, democracy, human rights and the roles of global citizenship.

'I realised that there is a need to be proactive in the community and society and that I need to have a high level of awareness with everything around me; I also feel the need to increase my level of flexibility and adaptability for the programme.'

'The programme has developed my understanding of issues that occur in many places globally. Poverty, conflict, hunger and lack of resources are world issues. Places are linked as they share the causes of and remedies to such issues.'

WHAT DOES 'GLOBAL CITIZENSHIP' MEAN TO YOU?

In our interviews, we also asked volunteers what global citizenship meant to them. Here are some of the responses:

'For me, we are talking about world citizens and what the common good is and what it is that I am doing here in South Africa that will affect somebody in London either directly or indirectly. World citizenship is therefore acknowledging that wherever we are, we have a relationship of some kind.'

'People working within different communities who are willing to learn and to share skills and respect and understand each other's opinions.'

'I see a global citizen as a person having a global awareness, global understanding of a cross-cutting global issue or problem. Being a global citizen would be not resting on an understanding or being content with an understanding but putting this understanding into relevant action, looking at where the opportunity presents itself.'

'It means sharing experiences, changing perceptions, challenging stereotypes. But if it just stops there it isn't global citizenship. Using that learning and putting it into action, influencing someone, changing someone, having a positive impact on the community – that's global citizenship.'

'Global citizenship is about a regional awareness linked to an understanding of where we sit in the globe.'

'Global citizenship means doing something to commit yourself to the wider community and contributing to the people's and the planet's well-being. There is a governmental, institutional element involved and it is a response to globalisation.'

'Considering oneself part of international communities with rights and responsibilities; being "world wise".'

'Being a global citizen is doing many little things that add up. You may not think that it is a big thing but actually it does really make a difference, even though it does not seem like it.'

'For me, when I say I am a global citizen, I come with no barriers. You look at the world not as your own but as something that belongs to all of us. I feel that I am a global citizen and what is right is what I am meant to do wherever I find myself. The barrier is not my passport; it is having that motivation to do whatever is right wherever I find myself.'

Does global citizenship then entail a formal relationship with a world government? In a society where the concept of world government has no official currency, that is a difficult question to answer.

Citizenship is the status of having the right to participate and to be represented in politics. Across the world and throughout history, many groups and communities have fought and organised themselves to gain citizenship rights. For example, the pursuit of universal suffrage was a dominant struggle throughout modern Europe during the late 19th and early 20th centuries.

The securing of legal and political rights has given legitimacy to government and is considered to have aided the stability of communities. It has often been the collective struggle itself that has brought people together as a community. Indeed, a community can be considered an association of people who are linked by common ideas, values, interests and objectives.

Communitarian theorists argue that being a citizen necessitates a level of civic engagement. The future of our community is secured only if we engage with other citizens and actively participate in the political process. Such a notion of an 'active citizenship' seems particularly pertinent today where our world is being transformed by the process of globalisation. These theories emphasise that citizenship brings with it responsibility and obligations to other members of the community.

However, this should not mean that we do not forget our responsibilities or obligations to those outside our community. This brings us to the notion of a universal 'global citizenship'; a citizenship that does not exclude any individuals or groups, and which reflects and addresses the erosion of national conceptions of community and citizenship.

The possible development of a global society as a consequence of globalisation has inevitably led to discussions about global citizenship and global civic engagement. Some have argued for a 'cosmopolitan' conception of global citizenship where individuals and groups from different societies unite to influence the global political agenda. The new social movements have been vehicles for such transnational political struggles. International non-governmental organisations have also been developed in response to the emerging global social and economic issues and problems.

Communitarian theorists criticise the cosmopolitan vision and argue that citizenship is based on nation-based rights and responsibilities. No citizenship at a global level could overcome the strong bond between the citizen and the nation state.

> **Доброволческа работа (Dobrovolcheska rabota)**
> Goodwill; voluntary work
> BULGARIA

Such debates about the future shape of communities are inevitable and reflect the broader arguments about the impact of globalisation. What is evident is that we need to engage actively in world politics as global citizens in order to bring people of the world together and play an active part in addressing the issues and problems that affect us all.[41]

Therefore, when we want to comprehend the concept of global citizenship, we need to not only be clear about our own understanding of citizenship, but also the challenges and changes globalisation brings to this understanding. But whatever the results of this may be, a binding principle for all global citizens is the belief that:

'The form globalisation takes is not inevitable and we can make choices about its direction. This is the singly most important premise of global citizenship and that of most self-styled global citizens: *that individuals can make a difference.*'[42]

Shramdan
Donation of labour
INDIA

Global governance

The call for action on a wider scale has intensified over recent years. Small actions do make a big difference; a house can only be built one brick at a time. But these small actions put together need to account for more than merely the sum of its parts. Many global issues – climate change, relative poverty and hunger – are unprecedented in their scale and magnitude. They need international co-ordinated efforts and structures in order to be addressed and eliminated. The UN Millennium Development Goals can be achieved only through international co-operation. Thus, often when talking of global citizenship, the term

---

CITIZENSHIP AND EUROPEAN HISTORY

As one example of how we come to a culturally specific understanding of citizenship, here is a small history of the evolution of citizenship in a European context:

'Citizenship' is the position of having the right to political participation and representation. It is linked to the concept of 'community' because it concerns the rights and obligations an individual acquires through membership of their community, whether in local, regional, national or global terms. Citizenship and community can be considered as interdependent, as the *raison d'être* of a community is to protect these rights and to impose these obligations, and at the same time, citizens must also uphold their obligations and defend their rights, and respect the rights of others, in order to maintain the community.

However, as always in politics, there are different and conflicting notions of community and citizenship. Such differences often reflect a difference in priority given to either the protection of individual rights or to the obligations to the community. For example, the liberal notion of citizenship prioritises individual rights, but the communitarian notion prioritises obligations and the pursuit of the 'common good'.

The liberal notion also reflects a more 'passive' notion of citizenship while the communitarian notion advances a more 'active' citizenship. The concept of an active citizenship implies working towards the development of the community for the benefit of all citizens through, for example, public service or volunteering. Passive citizenship tends to involve only the public activity of voting in elections.

The first forms of citizenship were active and involved obligations. Initially conceived by Aristotle (384–322 BC), citizenship reflected the way of life of the small, organic communities (the *polis*) of Ancient Greece. The *polis* were localised and tightly knit communities, where citizens (*polités*) had a strong sense of obligation towards their community and actively participated in running its affairs. Respecting the obligations towards the community was considered a virtue, and the active role of citizens made them governors of their own community.

'global governance' is invariably raised.

Global governance generally refers to the network of international governmental organisations, such as the United Nations, NATO or the European Union, but also international non-governmental organisations, for example pressure groups such as Amnesty International and Greenpeace; organisations that play a significant role in governing and shaping international politics.

The evolving system of global governance is increasingly complex because it operates at multiple levels – local, national, regional and global – and also includes participants that seek to achieve common transnational political goals or policy outcomes.

It is also a very loose political framework that consists of a wide variety of political, economic, social and cultural participants that influence politics at a supranational level. That is, all those who have the power to inform global changes in our policy, rules, values and attitudes.

However, citizenship in Ancient Greece was exclusive and unequal. It was based upon wealth, heritage and gender. Women and the poor were not considered citizens, and belonging to the *polis* was a birthright. Thus, citizenship was active but not democratic.

A more inclusive citizenship was considered virtuous with the rise of Christianity and secular absolutism in medieval Europe, which established the principle that everyone is equal in the eyes of God and the Sovereign who symbolised divine power on Earth. For St Augustine (AD 354–430), it was this equality of people in face of the will of God and the Sovereign that made them into citizens.

With the rise and expansion of the Roman Empire, a more passive form of citizenship developed. In great contrast to the small *polités* of Greece, the sheer size of the Roman Empire made active citizenship very difficult, but it was also undesired by the Roman state. Citizenship was more inclusive, but this was seen as a way of legitimising Roman rule and thus pacifying the conquered publics, as well as making it easier to collect taxes from them.

In democratic terms, the French Revolution (1789–99) and the declaration of human rights had a major impact on the notion of citizenship. It overturned the idea of citizenship where citizens were subjected to the will of God and the Absolute Monarchies and replaced it with a citizenship based upon universal rights.

The 'democratic revolution' that was ushered in by the French Revolution could be considered as incomplete because universal suffrage was not established until the 19th and early 20th centuries. As such, modern concepts of citizenship have been seen as intrinsically connected to the development of capitalism and the rise of the modern state and, in particular, the period of modernisation and industrialisation.

Gavin Moorhead

Global governance is also affected by a rise in transnational economic ties. Increasingly, our national economic policies are being informed by global economic forces and the goals of multinational corporations and such transnational bodies as the World Trade Organisation.

In cultural terms, rapid developments in technology, communication and transportation have realised the 1960s prophecy of the Canadian media commentator Marshall McLuhan of a 'global village', where people of the world are being brought closer together by the global information highway, supersonic travel and access to the same mass media. Indeed, it is such major changes in communication that are aiding the development of a global citizenship.

Such improvements in communication are also provoking social change. Increasing access to information from a variety of sources and different communities are influencing our social attitudes and broadening our horizons. Our social attitudes are also being influenced by a growing plurality of international social movements, which

SIERRA LEONE

Sierra Leone in West Africa is a country that has been shaped by upheaval since its independence in 1961. It has suffered from many military coups and an 11-year long, devastating civil war, which ended in 2002. The country is still suffering from the consequences of its recent history. It will probably take many more years for the country to recover, but this is the account of Kofi, a young volunteer from Ghana, who came to the area to help make a contribution to change:

'Sierra Leone was an interesting experience, seeing a country that was totally devastated by conflict and seeing people who felt that they could make a difference. It is not yet over, but if I look at the last two years and the training in leadership skills that we have done within the context of the organisation I went with to volunteer there, and see the lives that I have contributed to turning around perceptions in the military and the police, so that there would not be another conflict in Sierra Leone today, I feel proud that we are getting to where Africa should get to.

We did our training courses with representatives from the Republic of Sierra Leone's Armed Forces (RSLAF) and Sierra Leone Police (SLP) and civil society, represented by Hope-Sierra Leone (HSL). We started off working with the junior officers and then we moved on to training the senior officers. The commander-in-chief of the military has been through the programme himself, so very senior ranks in the military and police were there for the training. Before the elections, we did training for the presidential candidates, as well as youth officers and very senior ranks in the political parties. In a way, we have tried to cover women, youth, and men in general as well.

Now we are going to focus on what we call 'youth empowerment', where some volunteers are going to look at giving skills to young people to reintegrate them into society. I am basically focused on also giving what I call 'ethical empowerment' because I feel that you can always train people to have skills but the skills can be misused. To me, the original use of the term 'empowerment' is 'consciencisation'. For me, that is the basis for empowerment. You make people conscious of the fact that you can make money but without being greedy – make money in a genuine way and enjoy it as you wish, and also caring for other people while you make your money so that the environment and people around you benefit as well.

The last time I was in Sierra Leone, we had very senior political leaders come in and two political candidates. Initially they were not very comfortable. It was four days of training and at the end of the fourth day one of the very senior people in my community group, which was a relatively small group, said to me: 'Kofi, you do not know what you have done to us. You have put the dog, the cat, and the mouse in one room and we have not bitten each other.' For me, that was a turning point.

I feel that if today people in Sierra Leone can appreciate and go through a political process, vote for a president, and there is no war or other conflict, this is because such people have experienced changes in their life. If you look at what is happening in Kenya now, you can see what an election process can do to an African country, but Sierra Leone's election was, by and large, peaceful and for me that was what was needed.

I always say that I may not live to see the Africa I want to see, but if those junior officers in the police have started building up relationships and trust among the police and military and civil society in Sierra Leone, I have hope that one of the poorest countries in the world will one day become a beacon for Africa that everyone can learn from. That is one of the things that keeps me going back to Sierra Leone.'

transcend national borders and bring people together with similar goals, values and interests to change global politics through collective political action.

Different kinds of global citizenship

In his essay 'The Making of Global Citizenship', Richard Falk divides global citizens into five different categories: global performers, elite global business people, global environmental managers, politically conscious regionalists and transnational activists.[43] All these categories come with different assumptions of the role of the individual within their society. While elite global business people actively participate in the economic life in another country, they are unlikely to actively contribute to political and social life, as the time spent in these countries is often temporary.

In this book, we have already looked extensively at the ways in which civil society plays an important role as agent for change. Volunteers, alongside activists, advocates, community-based organisations, NGOs and other groups are involved in addressing global

Aikin Sa Kai
Working on your own will
NIGERIA

challenges. While the public sector has in most societies for a long time supported some notion of social welfare, the private sector has now increasingly become involved in advancing global betterment.

Corporate global citizenship

This is not an entirely new concept for the private sector; corporate philanthropy has been around even before industrialisation. But in recent years, the activities of corporate philanthropy have gained new momentum, both as a result of the consequences of doing business in a globalised world and pressure from civil society. Throughout the world, companies recognise the need not only to support charitable causes, but also to engage actively in social, political and humanitarian issues. They have therefore launched programmes based around what is generally called corporate social responsibility (CSR). The term refers to the activities that corporations participate in, besides their economic ones; activities that are aimed at improving social and political circumstances, such as health, poverty and the environment. CSR comes in many different guises, and companies keep developing new ways of becoming socially and environmentally responsible corporate global citizens.

Shachashabi
Voluntary; self-motivated during the floods; volunteer
BANGLADESH

The American ice cream manufacturer Ben & Jerry's is just as famous for its approach to corporate social responsibility as it is for ice creams. Since its foundation in 1978, the company has always had a strong focus on ethical business practices. The Ben & Jerry's Foundation, established in 1985, is responsible for distributing a small amount of the profits the company makes to community projects in the Vermont region, where Ben & Jerry's originated. Besides a high-quality product mission, the company states its social vision in its mission statement 'to operate the company in a way that actively recognises the central role that business plays in society by initiating innovative ways to improve the quality of life locally, nationally and internationally'.

Ben & Jerry's involvement in corporate social responsibility was not imposed by external pressures but resulted from the strong belief in ethical business practices. Other corporations have adapted socially and environmentally responsible strategies after receiving public or other pressures to do so.

For example, after the hanging of writer and human rights activist Ken Saro-Wiwa and eight other Ogoni activists in Nigeria in 1995, Shell have become engaged in environmental campaigns in the Niger Delta region. Shell had been generally criticised for its operations from sections of the local population, most notably the Ogoni people, but more particularly for condoning human rights abuses by the military government of Sani Abacha. Ken Saro-Wiwa is said to have been framed for his campaign to save the Niger Delta and the Ogoni people against the ecological repercussions of decisions made by the Nigerian government and Western oil corporations. In a press statement following the execution, Shell Nigeria reaffirmed its commitment to social and environmental issues by announcing that it would increasingly invest in ecologically more sustainable initiatives.

Since then, the face of major oil companies has changed dramatically. British Petroleum has promised to go to *beyond petroleum* in 2000; Shell are claiming to offset their CO_2 emissions by growing flowers and finding alternative, sustainable ways of operating their business; and ExxonMobil are supporting the 'Women Can' campaign, which is helping to develop leadership skills in African women.

CORPORATE GLOBAL CITIZENSHIP

The private sector has always been in some ways involved in promoting welfare and social change. Throughout history, these activities have been called different names, with an explosion of denominations having taken place over the past few decades. Corporate philanthropy has now often been replaced by its 'more modern' counterparts corporate responsibility, corporate social responsibility, citizenship brand, corporate citizenship, corporate global citizenship, business citizenship, ethical business, not-for-profit organisations, and inclusive business. Although all these terms carry slightly different assumptions and connotations, they are all ways that describe how businesses try to act in a more socially and ecologically responsible manner that benefits the people and the planet in a more sustainable way and in the long-term.

Although the impact of these changes is thought by many to be negligible, and the motivations of the companies little more than enlightened self-interest, they still reflect a change of attitude, and one that leads to the growth of more socially responsible business practices.

In a recent special report on corporate social responsibility, *The Economist* has stated that while it was 'once a do-gooding sideshow, [it] is now seen as mainstream'. The reasons for that are, according to the magazine: the increased pressure on corporations, mainly by NGOs, to report on their non-financial as well as on their financial results; the fact that climate change is probably the strongest driver for corporate social responsibility; and internal pressures, with an increasing demand for corporate social responsibility by employees. Corporations are now generally recognised as playing a broader role than the generation of economic capital. They are also assessed on ways in which they generate social capital and advance positive social change in their societies and globally. They are seen as major players in the discussion about global citizenship. [44]

Corporate global citizenship has pressured corporations into being more innovative in the ways in which they do business. Ben & Jerry's, BP, Shell and ExxonMobil are only a few examples where major companies have tried to incorporate socially and environmentally responsible strategies. This reflects the role that is assigned to the private sector in addressing global social injustice. Rather than being on the periphery of promoting social betterment, they are now actively involved, both for their resources, but also their resourcefulness.

Among other reasons, this results from the fact that corporate strategies can adapt the fast-paced global marketplace and its demands quicker than many public sector programmes. With their generation of large amounts of economic capital, they are in a powerful position that allows them to push forward a social and environmental agenda that has impact and potential influence. Furthermore, because economic development is based on and

> **Sain duriinhan**
> People giving free-will service
> MONGOLIA

THE TRIPLE BOTTOM LINE

The Triple Bottom Line has been introduced to measure success in the business world.
This means that many corporations are now measured by three distinct criteria:

- improved profits
- social performance
- ecological performance.

THE GRAMEEN BANK

The Grameen Bank was founded by Muhammad Yunus to provide small credits for people in deprived regions in Bangladesh. By giving mircocredits to the poorest, the Grameen Bank aims to lift people out of their poverty. For the development of their strategy and their efforts, Muhammad Yunus and the Grameen Bank were awarded the Nobel Peace Prize in 2006.

www.grameen-info.org

around innovation, private sector organisations are well-placed to lead in terms of sustainable development and social responsibility.

The Grameen Bank is one such development. In 2006, the Nobel Peace Prize was awarded to Professor Muhammad Yunus and the Grameen Bank, which he founded for the development and expansion of microcredit for impoverished entrepreneurs in deprived regions of Bangladesh and then the world.

The Noble Peace Prize Committee noted that instead of development programmes that concentrate on building up the wealth of a few people, the Grameen Foundation operates on the principle that: 'Lasting peace cannot be achieved unless large population groups find ways in which to break out of poverty. Microcredit is one such way. Development from below also serves to advance democracy and human rights.'[45] Over 90 per cent of the Grameen Bank loans are made to women; traditionally the economic power of woman has been ignored. Yet, in concentrating on raising the socio-economic status of women, you are ensuring that there is a greater impact on the community and the next generation. Loans are made to the individual, but the Grameen Bank also recognises the power of the community group. If a person is unable to fulfil payments, then the entire community is unable to receive any further loans. This encourages the whole community to help each other with repayments.

A major criticism of micro-finance is the privatisation of poverty, using market forces to further remove the state from issues of social welfare and economic regulation. This can be considered a positive means to strengthen societal cohesion or it can be viewed negatively as a way of reducing the control people have over their economic well-being. [46]

The Grameen Bank is an inclusive business, a model that is based on sustainable development by involving all members of a community, and one which aims especially to benefit low-income communities. All these business models attempt a more holistic way of development.

Consumer choices

One of the reasons for the rise in corporate social responsibility is the rise of ethical consumerism, which has spread all across the world, especially in the North. In the UK, for example, since 1999, the number of fair trade products sold has doubled every two years. Our own choice of consumer models can be an important aspect of global citizenship. Volunteering can help in playing an important role in the ways we consciously choose how we act as consumers. One of the volunteers we interviewed for this publication told us that volunteering had really made her realise how our everyday choices can affect and influence the lives of other people:

> 'But I suppose the most important change in myself was realising that little everyday choices in my life count. But what I have learned should not end there or in preaching to others. I learned I should couple learning with action – 'walk the talk'. So from choosing fair trade over non-fair trade products, choosing to 'bin it' not 'drop it', I realised that these everyday choices make good habits; make a lifestyle.'

Beyond affecting our consumer habits, volunteering also forms a more prominent role in global citizenship. As we have stated before, global citizens are aware that they are part of a wider community and

---

FAIR TRADE

It can be forgotten that the choices we make when buying food to eat or clothes to wear are not isolated events but can affect other people's lives dramatically. By eating a banana or drinking a cup of coffee you may be depriving a farmer of his or her ability to feed their own family. Although we like cheap and affordable food, it is the people who grew and produced the food who are paid less.

Supermarkets do not necessarily lose money when food is sold at half-price. The fair trade movement has gradually grown in influence over the last century, and uses an instantly recognisable logo that guarantees the food is grown to strict standards, ensuring that the people who produced the food are paid a living wage.

Food sold with the 'Fairtrade' logo may be more expensive, but it is recognised that the food is often of a higher quality and has been ethically grown, sold and resold. Small farmers are often more ecologically aware, as they are less likely to be able to afford expensive fertilisers and are more likely to employ ecologically sustainable methods such as growing in shade and using crop rotation.

By choosing Fairtrade over other products, consumers can therefore not only ensure farmers receive adequate payments for their produce, but also help slow down global climate change.

therefore that they share a responsibility with all other people to ensure the well-being of society as a whole. Through volunteering, people become more aware of the world around them and therefore learn to act more responsibly.

Volunteering and global citizenship

The importance of volunteering to global citizenship has also been recognised by the major corporations, who will now often allocate time or benefits to their volunteering staff. Many organisations from the North recognise the need to not only address issues in other countries, but also to be involved in volunteering in their own communities. As our global awareness of issues rises, so does the awareness of issues that affect our own communities. Only if we understand poverty, for example, on a global level, can we effectively address issues that relate to us at home. Whether it is volunteers from the chemist Boots helping in a breakfast club providing young schoolchildren in Birmingham with a meal in the morning, the Make an Impact on Tomorrow initiative by Henkel, Germany, which gives financial support to employees that volunteer and their projects, or Passion Days, which employees with Vodafone Australia are allowed to take in order to receive an additional day's paid leave when volunteering.

In our survey of global issues in this chapter, we might conclude that, before today, a citizen might have thought him- or herself a citizen of the world. The difference is that today this is not an effect of the individual imagination: we really are citizens of the world. As true cosmopolitans, we are demanding a new global governance and control of the world for the good of all. We increasingly look for a new configuration of forces, new social partnerships, which can rise to the challenges and opportunities that await us. This is something that will be shaped by the active citizens of today.

Endnotes

[40] Writers on these areas include Hans Küng, Martha Nussbaum, Kwame Anthony Appiah, James Clifford, Pnina Werbner and Homi K. Bhabha, who has proposed the term 'vernacular cosmopolitanism' in response to the debate

[41] Further reading: Dower, N. & Williams, J. (eds) (2002) *Global Citizenship: A Critical Reader*, Edinburgh: Edinburgh University Press
Held, D. (1995) *Democracy and the Global Order: From the Modern State to Cosmopolitan Governance*, Cambridge: Polity Press
Hutchings, K. & Dannreuther, R. (eds) (1999) *Cosmopolitan Citizenship*, London: Macmillan
Linklater, A. (2005) 'Globalization and the transformation of political community', in Baylis, J. & Smith, S. (2005) *The Globalisation of World Politics*, Oxford, Oxford University Press, pp. 709–725
Walzer, M. (1995) *The Defence of Pluralism and Equality*, Oxford: Blackwell

[42] Dower, N. *An Introduction to Global Citizenship*, Edinburgh: Edinburgh University Press, p.45

[43] Falk, Richard 'The Making of Global Citizenship' in: *The Condition of Citizenship*, Bart van Steenbergen (ed.), Sage Publications, London, 1994, reproduced with permission of Sage

[44] Franklin, Daniel 'Just good business', *The Economist*, 19 January 2008, The Economist Newspaper Limited, London

[45] http://nobelprize.org/nobel_prizes/peace/laureates/2006/press.html

[46] www.grameenfoundation.org
http://nobelprize.org/nobel_prizes/peace/laureates/2006/press.html
www.bangladeshnews.com.bd/2006/10/14/dr-muhammad-yunus-wins-nobel-prize-for-micro-credit
www.leftbusinessobserver.com/Micro.html

CHAPTER 5

THE
FUTURE

'March on. Do not tarry. To go
forward is to move toward
perfection. March on, and fear
not the thorns, or the sharp
stones on life's path.'

KAHLIL GIBRAN, 1883–1931

Volunteers planting trees in Multan, Pakistan. © VSO

THE FUTURE

'What you do today that is worthwhile
inspires others to act sometime in the future.'
MARCUS GARVEY, 1887–1940

This chapter, our final one, is about the future. Everyone who volunteers wants something to happen now. There is no such thing as a problem because when you recognise it you are already beginning to solve it. Today's problems, like poverty, rightly should belong to yesterday. The link between volunteering action and an immediate result is well established. But volunteers also seek organisations that will make the best of their efforts, that will organise them in the best way, and will help them learn. The best programmes will ensure personal development while building the best team. In Chapter 3, we surveyed different types of organisations and how they work. The stories of personal change throughout this book show how rewarding the results of volunteering can be. But most of these accounts are tempered by the challenge of sustaining the effort or making a long-lasting change.

> **Amarisachina**
> Bringing change
> GHANA

What does making a difference mean? A difference to what, with whose permission or collaboration and for how long? What are the kinds of long-lasting changes we want to see in the world? What questions do we need to ask of the future? What is the special kind of knowledge we need and where can we get it? Is there such a thing as the volunteering movement and if so, what is its future? When does the action of the group add up to more than the sum of its individual participants?

It seems that volunteering has entered a new era in which old ways of doing things are replaced by new patterns and structures. Traditional associations connected with volunteering, for example that of the 'old lady in the charity shop', are being replaced by a new wave of voluntary work. There has been a great increase in the volunteering movement over the last decades, not only in the amount of people involved in voluntary acts, but also in the number of possible volunteering opportunities.

So what of the future? As we have outlined in the book, new developments on a global scale have left a deep impact on our everyday lives. The rise of modern communication technology, for example, has made it much easier to expand our social and professional networks and to participate in societies far away from our own. This has

INVOLVING MORE PEOPLE IN VOLUNTEERING

Rousseau once said, 'everyone born in slavery is born for slavery'. So although we are essentially free, we are 'everywhere in chains'.[47]

Although there has been an increase in volunteering generally, which is perceived across the world, there are general tendencies of people more or less likely to be a part of this volunteering movement.

In England, for example, it seems that young men, especially young white men, are less likely to engage in voluntary work. This partly stems from the history of their society, which for a long time supported the notion of the male breadwinner, who feeds the family. While this traditionally has been a reason for more women to volunteer – they, after all, had more spare time to do benevolent work – it no longer holds true for today's society and work structures, where women are just as likely to pursue a career as men, where parental leave can be taken by fathers just as much as by mothers. That this specific sector of society does not play as important a role in volunteering therefore remains somewhat puzzling.

Another reason why young white men are less likely to volunteer has to do with the perception of the actual activities. Volunteering is by many people still seen as women knitting sweaters for their local church. It is perceived as an outdated concept, which lacks the vibrancy and attractiveness to interest young white men. But with volunteering opportunities as varied as they are today, from painting walls to being the front rider of a tandem bike, there is surely something for everyone.

A volunteer from Pakistan told us that in Pakistan it is mainly women who don't volunteer. Either, she says, because they are too involved in the home and therefore lack time or because cultural boundaries prevent it.

Besides, throughout the world, professionals are underrepresented in volunteering as their work times have increased and allow them a smaller amount of spare time to give. Usually, as young school leavers, people start to worry much more about their future and their careers, which takes precedence over most things. As volunteering in many modern societies is something that is done not as a responsibility but out of kindness, it is not perceived as a necessary part of being a member of society. Volunteering is not essential to everyday life; it is something you can do when you have time to fit it in.

As we have already said in Chapter 2, while some societies see volunteering as an act of kindness, others see it as a duty. The former are the ones these examples are taken from – they are the more individualistic societies that generally place more importance on personal development than on development as a community. In comparison, societies where social action is more a part of community life, volunteers have said that they cannot identify any particular groups who do not volunteer. In those societies, volunteering is very much a component of being a community member.

This shows that many of the reasons why people don't volunteer is because of the stigma that is attached to either the volunteers themselves or to the role different member societies attribute to volunteering. While these cannot be ignored, it is important to keep in mind that these restrictions are created by society and are not natural. So when we are considering whether to volunteer or not, we need to ask ourselves, what are the chains that are holding us back?

propelled the rise of civil society into new dimensions, and deeply unsettled global power relationships. Social action is now considered as forceful a tool in the global arena of influence as political or corporate decisions. Although the power of civic engagement has been proven throughout history, its global interconnectedness has given it new momentum, which cannot be framed by purely state-based mechanisms. This is also true for the ways in which governments run their countries and corporations do their business. It seems that the rise of a global network has also led to an increased global awareness. This in turn has resulted in checks and balances, which are happening on a much wider level.

Munca voluntara
Voluntary work
ROMANIA

Volunteering has changed dramatically as a result of these transformations. While previously, when volunteering took place, it was in a rather unco-ordinated, more or less arbitrary way. This has now changed. Revolutions in transport systems and communication technologies have facilitated the exchange of information and the sharing of good practice. This has very practical implications. A feminist NGO in Brazil can now look at the ways in which its Dutch counterpart campaigns for the same issues. It can get virtual and physical support through these new communication channels and therefore learn from other organisations' previous experiences. This has made it easier to ensure that campaigns are much more efficient and effective.

Similarly, societies can find inspiration in issues that are happening around the globe. A group in Northern England fighting for social cohesion in their own community may have been inspired by a community in Pakistan, who has found successful ways in overcoming its own fragmentation. This possibility of vibrant exchange between different people trying to achieve similar goals has led to a vast amount of innovation within the voluntary sector across the globe.

Bulungi bula nsi
Good for the country
UGANDA

Many of the problems the world is facing today are of a global nature. Therefore, to quote Kofi Annan, 'we need global blueprints to resolve these problems'. Many agents for social change have therefore recognised a need for increased international co-operation. Partnership is the decisive word when addressing issues such as poverty, hunger and climate change. Although all societies might face similar problems, they manifest themselves in different ways and to various extents in societies. Therefore it is important to work together with other partners to ensure that volunteering is targeted at the right people in the right ways. In volunteering terms, this means that the development of national volunteering is replacing the traditional North–South imbalance that has traditionally characterised the sector.

The future of volunteering lies in national volunteering, where local

ARMENIAN VOLUNTEER CORPS

Founded in 2000, the Armenian Volunteer Corps (AVC) calls on diasporan Armenians aged 21 and over (with no upper age limit) from around the world to volunteer their time, knowledge and energy to Armenia through a full immersion in living and working experience.

AVC matches the skills and interests of its volunteers with the needs of the country, with volunteer placements ranging from local NGOs, to hospitals, schools and small businesses for service terms as short as one month, to as long as one year.

The founder of AVC was a service-minded American–Armenian, who signed up to serve for the United States Peace Corps. Inspired by the way that long-term volunteer work allowed him and the other volunteers to connect deeply with the country and her people, their founder decided to create an organisation devoted to encouraging diasporans to connect with their ancestral homeland by working side by side with citizens of the country in a grand nation-building endeavour.

AVC strongly believes that the exchange of ideas, values, and experiences provides for mutual growth and understanding, and that the connection of human, informal, and capital resources of Armenians worldwide is the best way to help strengthen the country.

For instance, in 2006, a volunteer spent a portion of her time working with a community group in a village several hours south of the capital city Yerevan. She got to know the villagers as they developed a list of priorities for improving conditions in their community (such as clean water access, medical care, and renovations on their community centre) and then discussed actions they could take to meet their needs.

After she returned to the United States, she remained in touch with the villagers, and several months later heard that the World Bank had agreed to completely renovate their community centre, but only if the villagers contributed $2,500 as a cost share component. This, of course, was an impossible sum of money for the villagers to produce, or for her to donate by herself, but as a well-connected young professional in her own right, with access to other professionals and Armenian diasporans organisations, the 25-year-old volunteer was quick to see how she could be of assistance. Using the web to her and the village's benefit, she set up a fund online and sent out e-mails to people who might be interested in donating to the cause. Within days she had raised enough money for the villagers and wired the sum to the village. By mobilising her personal resources, she was able to make a huge impact on an entire village halfway around the globe. Construction on the community centre is to begin in 2007–08.

As a growing body of research and experience shows diasporans can play a significant role in the development of a nation (examples abound for Israel, Ethiopia, India, and Nigeria, among others), it becomes ever more clear that AVC's grass-roots nation-building model is a successful one.

Each person who has spent his or her life abroad, but then comes to Armenia to contribute his or her skills and ideas, is sowing the seeds of innovation that create more and more potential opportunities for the country's growth.

For many of the volunteers, having an Armenian background helps them feel profoundly connected with the country, and guarantees a vested interest in seeing the country succeed. It also helps provides an effective point of entry for building relationships with host families and the worksites.

A second-generation French–Armenian volunteer who spoke no Armenian prior to her arrival in the country recalls being amazed at how quickly her colleagues at the volunteer worksite entrusted her with a very critical project; at how her host family adopted her not as a visitor in their house but as a family member, right away; at how many people would shrug off their initial dismay at her inability to speak Armenian by saying 'ah, it doesn't matter – at least you have an Armenian soul'. The commonalities buffer the differences; the familiar helps pad the unfamiliar.

While a shared ethnic heritage helps create an emotional connection with Armenia, it is impossible to discount the realities of today's transnational world. AVC volunteers have lived most or all of their lives abroad and experience culture shocks to varying degrees upon arriving in Armenia. Whether they are from Argentina, Bulgaria, the UK or the USA, they carry certain nuances and belief systems born of their lives and experiences in those countries. This blending of cultural experience is eye-opening, both for AVC volunteers, and the friends they make in Armenia.

In effect, volunteers are the human faces of international diplomacy. For some local Armenians, particularly ones in rural areas, who spent 70 years under the Soviet system, designed to close out all foreign influence, volunteers are the first people they meet from the transnational world. The impression they make can bolster or instantly break down stereotypes that have been developed solely from television, media, and hearsay over the years.

In exchange, volunteers come to intimately understand the daily practicalities of what it means to be a 'developing nation' or a 'nation in transit'. It helps put meaning to previously vague concepts like 'rule of law', 'democratisation', 'foreign aid', 'economic development', 'sustainability' and beyond. It simply can't be avoided when one is living in a Stalin-era apartment building with a host family whose mother makes a living by working for a Canadian rural roads development project, while volunteering with an anti-corruption organisation, and keeping up with everyday chatter on the bus, which may be about the details of EU expansion and citizenship, or how a secret ballot system should work.

And finally, many volunteers spend their time in Armenia searching for some kind of identity affirmation. Many AVC volunteers are first, second, or third generation Canadians, or Brazilians who know very little about their historical roots, language and culture.

Thanks to technology and an integrated global economy, national borders are eroding at an unprecedented rate. Thus, many find it personally imperative to find a grounding in their own identity, which can help them navigate this age of globalisation.

The application process for AVC asks potential volunteers to write a motivational statement. A common theme in these statements is this very search for a connection with one's heritage. As an American–Armenian volunteer once beautifully articulated, she embarked on her journey to Armenia after coming to an understanding that negotiating between her cultural 'otherness' would always hinge on her understanding of the 'homeland'.

Anoush Rima Tatevossian

communities have an influence in the changes that affect them. It is well known that in order to create lasting change, it is important to involve the people concerned. Douglas Alexander, Secretary of State for International Development in the United Kingdom, gave a speech in which he stressed that development can be sustained only if the people are made a part of it. The UK government subsequently gave £3 million to support international volunteering among the diasporic population. Diasporic populations often need to balance a sense of belonging both to their countries of origin as well as their home countries, which can often be successfully juggled. If not, then it can lead to the kinds of situation where people are more likely to feel alienated within a society. Volunteering and its active involvement on a local level, has the potential to increase social cohesion in these communities.

This means that while international volunteering will still be important, local volunteers should be involved in the front line work and all possible barriers to participation should be removed. Also, to bridge gaps of understanding, a rise in volunteers from the South to help with issues in the North could be a way forward. Reciprocity is the critical word when engaging in long-term sustainable initiatives.

Just as important as international partnerships, is the co-operation between all three sectors in society. Already, volunteering is not confined to the third sector, with both public and private sector institutions finding ways of incorporating volunteering opportunities for their employees. The rise of civil society, the third force, as it is sometimes referred to, has compelled both public institutions and private corporations to keep up with global developments in these areas. This has led to a situation, where all sectors are actively involved in social action, volunteering, the promotion of social justice and equality, but all in their own, different ways. All three put together could be a very powerful tool for global betterment: the public sector through political support, funding and the provision of a structured framework, the private sector for its resources, flexibility and fast-paced adaptability and the third sector as a voice for the many and pool of human and social capital.

Faire du bénévolat
To have goodwill
FRANCE

When all three sectors find ways to effectively work together, this can have a huge impact on community cohesion overall. The more players are genuinely involved, the wider the reach of such programmes will be. This is a massive area of potential expansion for the voluntary sector in the future. Especially with an increasing number or businesses signing up for the social agenda – the triple bottom line – they meet their customers' demands while at the same time offering effective ways of development.

In order for the voluntary sector to remain an important player in positively influencing the global development agenda, it needs to embrace change. The work and lifestyle structure of modern affluent society is quite different from what it used to be. It may be a cliché to say it, but life has become more ephemeral and fast-paced. However, for the woman walking four hours a day to collect water in Darfur, time has its own agonising rhythm. For the cash-rich but time-poor citizen of a G8 nation, it passes in a blur. If views of the voluntary sector are outdated, then the sector itself needs to embrace change and be seen to do it.

What might this mean for the future? One of the underlying trends is the changing nature of paid work against which volunteering defines itself. In his book *The End of Work*, Jeremy Rifkin imagines a world where humans are left to fill in those areas of work that the machines they have designed cannot operate. There will be two groups of salaried workers: an elite of thinkers; and a just-in-time worforce of skilled manual workers. This will leave the majority of citizens free to contribute the essential human skills such as counselling, caring, parenting, educating and entertaining. These skills will be rewarded with various forms of social credit. Whether or not this scenario comes to pass, there are signs that the old world of work in developed nations is set to change.

The UK's Commission on the Future of Volunteering report – *Manifesto for Change* – recommends that employers find ways to reward staff who are involved in volunteering activities, not by financial payment, but by reducing their hours. They could, for example match the hours volunteered by a reduction in working hours. So, in thinking about volunteering, one also has to imagine how paid work might change in future. The scope for creative thinking is enormous as work, the traditional antithesis of leisure, is itself reinvented.

> *Tusitukilawamu*
> Support; get-up together
> UGANDA

Time and money are often perceived, whether true or not, as scarce resources that need to be shared thoughtfully. Volunteering organisations need to keep this in mind when they plan voluntary placements. With unemployment on the rise and increased pressures of kick-starting one's career as early as possible, potential volunteers need to be targeted in ways that reflect their lifestyles and their attitudes. Flexible, no-commitment volunteering opportunities have mushroomed in the last decade. Now it is a question of making these initiatives sustainable in order to permanently improve living conditions for the less advantaged around the world.

Internet-based social networking portals such as Facebook, Bebo and MySpace – the poster-boys of the so-called information communication technologies or ICTs – are revolutionising the way in which volunteering is operating in the 21st century. How many of us have received invitations to join groups bearing names such as 'Ciaran's big fat triathlon fund-raising extravaganza' and inviting us to pledge money to the cause?

This new way of raising sponsorship has all but consigned the good old-fashioned hard copy sponsorship forms to the wastepaper basket and it's only a short hop from this into the blossoming world of global volunteering programmes. As the activities of volunteers and the noble causes of their various projects, programmes and initiatives find a whole new global audience, the increasing scope of what can be achieved is only now becoming clear. More and more people are becoming exposed not only to the impact that such activities can have in the world, they are also, by way of blogs, testimonies, and photographic accounts, fuelling a whole new enthusiasm for what can be achieved.

A new generation of volunteers is emerging, who can see quite graphically the difference that they can make through their endeavours. This is because they can receive immediate feedback on the actions of people like themselves from all parts of society. They read about what people achieve, and their appetite for action is constrained only by the limitless possibilities of what can be accomplished. Although the actual voluntary activities themselves still take place in what might be termed 'the real world', the effect of those actions is multiplied a thousandfold through modern communications. The potential for sharing such experiences is reaching unprecedented levels.

It is chiefly for this reason that the attention afforded to volunteering-related ICT exposure among the business sector is becoming so significant. Always keen to reach greater and more diverse audiences, companies are frantically courting such connections in an attempt to tap into their popularity, particularly among the younger generations, and to exploit 'social capital' in new and dynamic ways. Whether or not this concept, described by Professor Ian Diamond, Chief Executive of the Economic and Social Research Council, as 'that reserve of goodwill generated by people's social interactions' is enriched or diminished by online vehicles is still the subject of some debate, organisations know that if they do choose to ignore it, they do so at their peril.

All of this means that more and more money is pouring into the voluntary sector as the business case for corporate social responsibility is universally embraced. Although money for more traditional forms of charity is by no means disappearing, it is increasingly being diverted into what are seen as projects with a wider social benefit for

Tūao

Work for a time; work as a volunteer
NEW ZEALAND (MAORI)

A volunteer supports her host home's shoe-making business.

all of those involved. Money is becoming available from all sectors as the private and public sectors interact. Money from government, grants from bodies such as the National Lottery Commission, not to mention funding from the EU and other supranational organisations, all further strengthen the financial position of volunteer organisations and the activities they carry out.

At the same time, the world is shaped by a digital divide, with many people not able to access information and communication technology as easily as others. It is one of the challenges we need to consider when we want to make our strategies and approaches have a lasting effect. We need global structures available so that people can channel their energies into positive action. Although the internet offers the possibility of providing these, they are often not organised and don't reach those people who do not have online access and do not speak English.

Sarwar Bari, National Co-ordinator for Pattan in Pakistan, suggested a Global Youth Parliament for returned volunteers. In connection to Global Xchange, he suggested that each team elected a woman and a man for a certain number of years. These elected volunteers would then convene twice a year, rotating between each participating country with a different agenda that is set by each of the countries. This could then lead to an increased exchange of experience and sharing of best practice, initiated by different countries, to allow an equal representation of their ideas. This scheme could be extended to other organisations and even more countries.

Thabo Putu from South Africa also suggested the importance of a structured and organised approach and the flexibility to adapt to

Pagkukusa
Initiative
PHILIPPINES

changes as a major aspect in the future of the volunteering sector. He pointed out the importance of learning from each other, something he had experienced on a recent study tour to the Philippines. The ways in which Filipinos manage to incorporate their professional lives with their volunteering activities has been an inspiration to how the University of Witwatersrands conducts its own volunteering programme.

The way volunteering is organised depends on two levels. On the one hand, volunteering needs to become more local, with community-based organisations setting the agenda of how volunteers will be needed and how they will be put into action within their community. They are best-placed to know the typical traits of that community, they have the trust of the locals, and they just know the community well. Therefore, they are the most appropriate people to make decisions on what and how things happen on the local level.

On the other hand, the organisation of volunteering will need to become more global in order to maximise the contributions of volunteers. It will require some sort of global management, or global governance that will provide the necessary structures for volunteering on a global level, so that it becomes a more co-ordinated effort. Global structures are necessary to create platforms of exchange, information, resources and knowledge that can be a hub for volunteers, volunteering organisations and any other participant who is interested in furthering social change. These platforms must also include former volunteers whose influential advocacy and expertise should be encouraged rather than neglected. Only through the provision of knowledge, the sharing of best practice and the creation of sustained networks can volunteering organisations learn from others and improve their own operations on a local level.

The new local–global formation as outlined above and the increasing reciprocity of volunteering, where volunteering is less about one-way instruction, but rather a genuine two-way reciprocal act, which involves and benefits both sides, has also led to an increase in cross-cultural exchanges. As we become increasingly aware of the diversity, and also the commonalities that bind us together as humans, intercultural competencies become a crucial tool for people to have.

The ways in which we engage with people from other cultures can become strong indicators of whether the work will be successful or not. These necessary intercultural skills, so pivotal in the 21st century, require every one of us to be culturally aware not just of someone else's way of living but also able to recognise our own idiosyncrasies as part of a specific sociocultural group. Through international volunteering, we can gain important insights into how to address diversity and overcome

Etu hoa kya
Volunteer
GHANA (FANTE)

difference. The more we are exposed to other ways of thinking, the more we will be capable of finding solutions to potential intercultural hotspots.

As more and more people recognise the need to actively engage in the world's multifarious events, they realise that volunteering is not just a choice of how to spend our free time, it is part of a lifestyle: the lifestyle of an active global citizen. This not only includes addressing those issues that require social action, it also involves the ways in which we inform ourselves about what happens to people all over the world, and recognise that we are all linked by one common bond, our humanity. As local actions can have a tremendous impact on a global scale, we need to think global when we are acting local.

Our consumption choices matter, because they affect people in other societies much more now – because of economic integration through globalisation – than they did a few decades ago. But this is not just a question of whether or not to buy fair trade and organic foods and clothes from ethical businesses. Rather than just paying to offset our carbon footprint when we are flying, we should ask ourselves how necessary that flight really is? Do I recycle, or do I try to find ways in which to reduce the production of waste? Do I buy energy-saving light bulbs or do I pay attention to not leaving more lights on than necessary? We need to reflect on what we are doing every day – only if each and every one of us rethink how we lead our lives, can we help make the world a better place for the masses, rather than just a lucky few.

Also, when we think about what we can do, we don't need to look at the other side of the world. Volunteering and social action can become much more ingrained in our everyday lives. Do we help our neighbour to carry shopping bags? Do we help a lost person find his or her way? Do we bake a cake for a fund-raising event at our child's school? No matter how small these actions are perceived to be, they still make a difference. These small actions put together can make a major difference to the lives of others. If volunteering is to increase its impact, then more people need to be convinced of the fact that even if they can give only an hour a week, they will contribute to positive social change. It is not necessarily about how long and how well we do things, it is our willingness to do something – anything.

It would be wrong to finish this book in any way other than by hailing the tremendous impact that volunteers continue to have in the world. So, no matter how small your contribution, how seemingly insignificant your actions, just go out and do something. You'll be amazed at what a difference you can make. This is nicely, if not over-elaborately illustrated by a colleague in his rendition of popular Southern African anecdote:

Paglilingkod
Service
PHILIPPINES

'Picture a scene on a beach, the hot midday sun beating down upon the sands. Out in the surf, see brightly coloured fish hurling themselves out of the water, their rainbow scales glistening in the sunlight, and hear the hiss as they hit the scorching sand, and wriggle, writhe and flip in futile realisation that jumping out of the water really was a bad idea. Amid the suicidal orgy of dying fish, a small boy is frantically scooping up the slippery, gasping, expiring little bodies and flinging them back into the ocean. One by one. But still they come, perhaps the same ones, perhaps new ones, flying out towards him. People begin to congregate on the beach to watch this strange drama unfold. Some begin to laugh at the boy in his seemingly futile efforts, mocking him and questioning what difference he thinks he is making, since all around him fish are dying. The boy is unabashed. As he throws fish after fish back into the crashing surf he turns to his detractors, defiantly telling them that no matter how many fish perish, if even one fish swims away to safety, it will make his actions worthwhile a hundred times over. Confounded by the simplicity and fierce sincerity of his words, the crowd disperse, leaving the unlikely hero to continue with his work unmolested.'

Endnotes

[47]   Rousseau, Jean-Jacques, *The Social Contract*, Penguin, 1968

DIRECTORY OF VOLUNTEERING ORGANISATIONS

DIRECTORY OF
VOLUNTEERING ORGANISATIONS

UK-based

Book Aid International

Book Aid International promotes literacy in developing countries by creating reading and learning opportunities for disadvantaged people. It recruits volunteer book collectors to transport donated books to their premises in Camberwell. Volunteers also work in the library/warehouse to help sort and pack the books shipped annually to its partners in sub-Saharan Africa. It also needs volunteers for general administration. Opportunities also arise for internships for assistance on specific projects.

39–41 Coldharbour Lane, Camberwell, London SE5 9NR
Telephone +44 (0)20 7733 3577
E-mail volunteering@bookaid.org
www.bookaid.org

British Council

The British Council is the UK's international organisation for cultural relations and educational opportunities. Through the ties that it creates between people in the UK and other countries, it helps to build lasting relationships and break down barriers to understanding. It also aims to increase appreciation of the UK's creative ideas and achievements. This work is driven by its strong belief in internationalism and the conviction that cultural relations can help individuals and the world community to thrive. It develops programmes on learning, arts, science and society and is a partner of Global Xchange.

10 Spring Gardens, London SW1A 2BN
General enquiries +44 (0)161 957 7755
Minicom +44 (0)161 957 7188
E-mail general.enquiries@britishcouncil.org
www.britishcouncil.org

British Trust for Conservation Volunteers (BTCV)

BTCV is the UK's leading practical environmental conservation charity, providing volunteering opportunities, holidays, training courses and leadership courses for all age groups throughout the UK and overseas.

Sedum House, Mallard Way, Doncaster DN4 8DB
Telephone +44 (0)1302 388 883
E-mail information@btcv.org.uk
www.btcv.org

Community Service Volunteers (CSV)

Community Service Volunteers (CSV) is the UK's largest volunteering and training charity. It was founded in 1962 by Mora and Alec Dickson, who also founded VSO. Its philosophy is that everyone should be able to take part in the life of their community. Its aim is to involve young people aged 16 to 35 in the voluntary service, to enrich the lives of volunteers and those they help, and to generate social change. In 2007, the CVS involved nearly 250,000 people in volunteering in the UK and trained 12,000 disadvantaged young people.

237 Pentonville Road, London N1 9NJ
Switchboard +44 (0)20 7278 6601
E-mail information@csv.org.uk
www.csv.org.uk

Concordia

Concordia provides young people with opportunities for international volunteering, work experience, education and training. It is part of a worldwide network of partner organisations that have developed a system of volunteer exchange.

19 North Street, Portslade, Brighton BN41 1DH
Contact details for the European Voluntary Service (EVS) programme are:
Telephone +44 (0)1273 425513
E-mail fiona@concordia-iye.org.uk
www.concordia-iye.org.uk

Contact details for the international programme are:
Telephone +44 (0)1273 422218
E-mail info@concordia-iye.org.uk

Contact details for the UK programme are:
Telephone +44 (0)1273 422535
E-mail helenpheasey@concordia-iye.org.uk

Frontier

Frontier recruits volunteers for research and development projects aimed at safeguarding biodiversity and ecosystem integrity, and building sustainable livelihoods for marginalised communities in the world's poorest countries.

50–52 Rivington Street, London EC2A 3QP
Telephone +44 (0)20 7613 2422
E-mail info@frontier.ac.uk
www.frontier.ac.uk

Global Xchange

Global Xchange is a partnership programme managed and delivered by the British Council, VSO and a number of local partners around the world. Active global citizenship is at the heart of the programme and its vision is to build a world where active global citizens create positive change and build mutual understanding and respect.

The programme comprises bilateral and recently introduced regional international volunteering exchanges, which bring together volunteers aged between 18 and 25 years old from the UK and overseas countries. They have an opportunity to learn more about themselves, and each other, to work for positive change, and to bring benefits to local communities in the UK and overseas. This is achieved by them living and working in host communities in the UK and overseas for a period of six months, and also comprises community exchanges, which strengthen leadership skills, and cross-cultural understanding. The programme promotes active participation of young people in communities; showcases the benefits of community cohesion; builds new active networks and dialogues; promotes positive social action; and provides tools to measure the impact of community initiatives.

Global Xchange, c/o VSO, 317 Putney Bridge Road, London SW15 2PN
Telephone +44 (0)20 8780 7500
E-mail enquiry@globalxchange.org.uk
www.globalxchange.org.uk

GO London

Organised by Community Service Volunteers (CSV), GO London offers easy and commitment-free volunteering opportunities for people in London.

Telephone +44 (0)20 7643 1341
E-mail gocity@csv.org.uk
www.csv.org.uk/go

Groundwork

Groundwork supports communities in need and promotes economic and social regeneration by improving the local environment. Its vision is of a society of sustainable communities that respect the local and global environment and where individuals and enterprise prosper.

Lockside, 5 Scotland Street, Birmingham B1 2RR
Telephone +44 (0)121 236 8565
E-mail info@groundwork.org.uk
www.groundwork.org.uk

International Voluntary Service (IVS) GB

IVS GB is a peace organisation working for the sustainable development of local and global communities throughout the world. It is the leading charity involving volunteers in international exchanges. IVS GB is the British branch of Service Civil International (SCI), a worldwide network supporting the mutual exchange of volunteers to work on projects of direct benefit to local communities.

IVS regional offices:
IVS England: Oxford Place Centre, Oxford Place, Leeds LS1 3AX
Telephone +44 (0)113 246 9900
Fax +44 (0)113 246 9910
E-mail england@ivs-gb.org.uk
E-mail youthwork@ivs-gb.org.uk
www.ivs-gb.org.uk

IVS Scotland: Thorn House, 5 Rose Street, Edinburgh EH2 2PR
Telephone +44 (0)131 243 2745
Fax +44 (0)131 243 2747
E-mail scotland@ivs-gb.org.uk

IVS Northern Ireland: 122 Great Victoria Street, Belfast BT2 7BG
E-mail colin@ivsni.co.uk

Lattitude Global Volunteering

Lattitude Global Volunteering specialises in volunteering for 17- to 25-year-olds. It has a global vision and aims to provide a unique experience of voluntary work placements for young people from around the world. It places volunteers in Africa, Asia, the Americas, Europe, and Australasia, and offers a variety of placements including teaching, caring, environmental, outdoor activity, medical and community development projects.

Head office (including UK and European volunteers):
44 Queen's Road, Reading, Berkshire RG1 4BB
Telephone +44 (0)118 959 4914
E-mail volunteer@lattitude.org.uk
www.lattitude.org.uk

Australian volunteers:
Gap Activity Projects Australia, PO Box 6054, Chapel Street North, South Yarra, Victoria 3141
Telephone +61 (0)3 9826 6266
E-mail enquiries@gapactivityprojects.org.au

New Zealand volunteers:
Gap NZ, PO Box 4134, Manawatu Mail Centre, Palmerston North, 4442
Telephone +64 (0)6 350 5920
E-mail gapnz@xtra.co.nz

Mencap

Mencap is the UK's leading learning disability charity. It believes that everyone has gifts and, by giving time and effort, has something special to offer by volunteering. It provides many opportunities for volunteering including at one-off events, volunteering alongside a person with a learning disability and regular volunteering at one of their local groups.

123 Golden Lane, London EC1Y 0RT
Telephone +44 (0)845 123 3000
E-mail volunteering@mencap.org.uk
www.mencap.org.uk/volunteer

National Trust

The National Trust preserves and protects the coastline, countryside and buildings of England, Wales and Northern Ireland. It offers an opportunity to get involved in conservation work and offers full-time, employee, and youth involvement programmes as well as working holidays.

National Trust Central Volunteering Team, The National Trust, Heelis, Kemble Drive, Swindon SN2 2NA
Telephone +44 (0)1793 817632
E-mail volunteers@nationaltrust.org.uk
www.nationaltrust.org.uk

Prince's Trust

The Prince's Trust is the UK's leading youth charity and helps to change young lives. They give practical and financial support to 14- to 30-year-olds, enabling them to develop skills that will help them move into education and training.

18 Park Square East, London NW1 4LH
Telephone +44 (0)20 7543 1234 or 0800 842 842
E-mail info@princes-trust.org.uk
www.princes-trust.org.uk

Project Trust

Project Trust is an educational charity that sends volunteers overseas between school and university or employment, and is widely respected as one of the most experienced and professional gap year organisations in Britain.

Project Trust on Isle of Coll:
The Hebridean Centre, Isle of Coll, Argyll PA78 6TE
Telephone +44 (0)1879 230444
E-mail info@projecttrust.org.uk

Project Trust in London:
12 East Passage, Long Lane, London EC1A 7LP
Telephone +44 (0)207 793 1173
E-mail info@projecttrust.org.uk
www.projecttrust.org.uk

The Simon Community

The Simon Community helps homeless people and offers an alternative to institutional care. It aims to help people who are not provided for by other services and seeks to break down barriers between helping and being helped. Its residents and volunteers live and work together as a community and share in the decision-making and running of all its projects.

129 Malden Road, Camden, London NW5 4HS
Telephone +44 (0)20 7485 6639
E-mail info@simoncommunity.org.uk
www.simoncommunity.org.uk

Student Partnerships Worldwide (SPW)

SPW is an international non-governmental organisation that recruits and trains young people (aged 18 to 28) as Volunteer Peer Educators to lead programmes that address urgent health and environmental issues in Africa and Asia.

205–207 Davina House, 137–149 Goswell Road, London EC1V 7ET
Telephone +44 (0)20 7490 0100
E-mail info@spw.org
www.spw.org

Student Volunteers Network

The Student Volunteers Network is for students from across the country to get together and share their passion and enthusiasm for volunteering.

www.svnetwork.ning.com

Sudan Volunteer Programme (SVP)

The SVP sends graduates and undergraduates to Sudan to teach English at schools, colleges and universities. Its main objectives are to promote the exchange of cultures and to develop lifelong links.

34 Estelle Road, London NW3 2JY
Telephone +44 (0)20 7485 8619
E-mail david@svp-uk.com
www.svp-uk.com

Thrive

Thrive uses gardening as a way of changing the lives of disabled people. It aims to show how, why and where people with a disability can benefit by gardening through its research, education and promotional activities. Volunteers can work directly with clients alongside therapists; look after visitors during the weekend; help with open days; help with fund-raising activities, and provide administrative support. There are also opportunities for corporate volunteering.

The Geoffrey Udall Centre, Beech Hill, Reading, Berkshire RG7 2AT
Telephone +44 (0)118 988 5688
E-mail via website
www.thrive.org.uk

TimeBank

TimeBank, the national volunteering charity, tackles social issues by finding ways for people to give their time that inspire them and match their lives. It also helps charitable organisations and businesses develop innovative and effective volunteer programmes.

2nd Floor, Downstream Building, 1 London Bridge, London SE1 9BG
Telephone +44 (0)845 456 1668
E-mail info@timebank.org.uk
www.timebank.org.uk

Tools for Self Reliance

Tools for Self Reliance works to help relieve poverty in Africa, focusing on the artisan sector in rural communities. Volunteers help collect and refurbish tools in the UK and work to raise awareness about the causes of poverty. They welcome volunteers from a wide range of backgrounds.

Netley Marsh, Southampton, Hampshire SO40 7GY
Telephone +44 (0)23 8086 9697
E-mail info@tfsr.org
www.tfsr.org

UNA Exchange

UNA Exchange provides a range of volunteering throughout Wales and the rest of the world. It promotes and supports international understanding, cultural exchange and community development as well as enabling volunteers' personal growth and development. UNA Exchange volunteers always work in partnership with local community groups.

The Welsh Centre for International Affairs, Temple of Peace, Cathays Park, Cardiff CF10 3AT
Telephone +44 (0)29 2022 3088
E-mail unaexchange@btinternet.com
www.unaexchange.org

Universities' Trust for Educational Exchange with Palestinians (Unipal)

Unipal facilitates a two-way process of education by providing English language teaching in Palestinian refugee camps in the West Bank, Gaza and Lebanon and gives British students the opportunity of acquiring a knowledge and understanding of the situation and daily lives of refugees.

BCM Unipal, London WC1N 3XX
Telephone +44 (0)208 299 1132
E-mail info@unipal.org.uk
www.unipal.org.uk

V

V is an independent youth volunteering charity that seeks to inspire young volunteers in England and enable lasting change in the quality, quantity and diversity of youth volunteering. Its aim is to create a culture where it is natural for young people to volunteer and natural for organisations to support them in doing so.

5th Floor, Dean Bradley House, 52 Horseferry Road, London SW1P 2AF
Telephone +44 (0)20 7960 7000
E-mail via website
www.wearev.com

Vitalise

Vitalise provides short breaks (respite care) and other services for disabled and visually impaired people, and carers. Volunteers are recruited as sighted guides (and get a subsidised holiday) or take part in fund-raising events. Volunteers also work in Vitalise centres and shops, and there are group, team, community and home-sharer volunteer programmes.

Shap Road Industrial Estate, Shap Road, Kendal, Cumbria LA9 6NZ
Telephone +44 (0)845 330 0148
E-mail volunteer@vitalise.org.uk

Outside UK:
Telephone +44 (0)1539 814 682
E-mail overseasvolunteer@vitalise.org.uk
www.vitalise.org.uk

Volunteering England

Volunteering England is committed to supporting, enabling and celebrating volunteering in all its diversity. Its work links research, policy innovation, good practice and grant making in the involvement of volunteers.

Regents Wharf, 8 All Saints Street London N1 9RL
Telephone +44 (0)845 305 6979
E-mail volunteering@volunteeringengland.org
www.volunteering.org.uk

Volunteers for Sri Lanka (VESL)

VESL was established to develop volunteering opportunities in Sri Lanka, India and Thailand. It provides children at rural schools with the opportunity to learn from enthusiastic and creative native English speakers.

19 Bryson Road, Polworth, Edinburgh EH11 1ED
Telephone +44 (0)845 094 3727
E-mail info@vesl.org
www.vesl.org

VSO

VSO is an international charity that promotes volunteering to overcome global poverty and disadvantage. It responds to requests for volunteers from governments and community organisations throughout Asia and Africa, and it has become the most prominent international development charity that works with volunteers. In the 2004 Charity Awards, it won the International Aid and Development category for its promotion of innovative approaches to globalising volunteering.

It recruits volunteers for a broad range of work, including teachers, social workers, health professionals, management consultants, marine biologists, business advisers, accountants and farmers. The strategy is for volunteers to pass on their expertise to local people so that these skills remain after the volunteers have left. It thus contributes to sustainable development.

317 Putney Bridge Road, London SW15 2PN
Volunteering Advice Line +44 (0)20 8780 7500 (Monday to Friday, 0900–1700)
E-mail enquiry@vso.org.uk
www.vso.org.uk
Frequently asked questions *www.vso.org.uk/volunteering/faq*

WorkingAbroad

WorkingAbroad provides an easily accessible network of information to help people find careers in environmental and humanitarian fields of work.

The Old School House, Pendomer, Yeovil, Somerset BA22 9PH
Telephone +44 (0)1935 864 458
E-mail info@workingabroad.com
www.workingabroad.com

World Service Enquiry

The World Service Enquiry provides overseas placements, information and career advice to people who want to volunteer or work in international aid and development at home, or overseas in the developing world. Its services and information solutions aim to inform and enable people to contribute to the global community.

237 Bon Marché Centre, 241–251 Ferndale Road, London SW9 8BJ
Telephone +44 (0)870 770 3274
E-mail wse@wse.org.uk
www.wse.org.uk

WorldWide Volunteering (WWV)

WorldWide Volunteering aims to make it easier for people of all ages to volunteer through its database, which enables volunteers to build an on-screen profile of their ideal placement, which is then matched against the needs of organisations in the UK and worldwide.

7 North Street Workshops, Stoke sub Hamdon, Somerset TA14 6QR
Telephone +44 (0)1935 825588
E-mail wwv@wwv.org.uk
www.wwv.org.uk

Youth for Development (YfD)

Youth for Development is a one-year VSO programme that provides an opportunity for young people to become involved in overseas development work and the promotion of international understanding. It offers young volunteers, aged 18 to 25, a chance to use their skills and to make a tangible contribution to fighting poverty.

317 Putney Bridge Road, London SW15 2PN
Telephone +44 (0)208 780 7500
E-mail enquiry@vso.org.uk
www.vso.org.uk/volunteering/youth

UK- and overseas-based

Amnesty International

Amnesty International is a worldwide movement of people who campaign for internationally recognised human rights for all. Its headquarters, the International Secretariat in London, runs a voluntary programme where it currently receives the support of 100 to 115 volunteers and interns. Volunteers help members of staff with all aspects of their work and are involved in all programmes across the International Secretariat. Amnesty say that the support they get from volunteers and interns is invaluable and that they could not function without them. Cultural diversity is an important factor in Amnesty International's success, and something they work to increase. As such, they invite all applicants to visit their website for volunteering and internship opportunities.

1 Easton Street, London WC1X 0DW
Telephone +44 (0)20 7413 5500
www.amnesty.org/en/jobs_all/volunteer-opportunities

Cross-Cultural Solutions (CCS)

CCS delivers three international volunteer programmes: Volunteer Abroad (its flagship programme), Intern Abroad (a one-week international volunteering programme) and Insight Abroad (for students interested in having an international internship or earning academic credit). These programmes are designed to balance volunteer work, cultural and learning activities and free time.

Headquarters:
2 Clinton Place, New Rochelle, New York 10801, USA
Telephone 1 800 380 4777, 1 914 632 0022
E-mail info@crossculturalsolutions.org

Canada:
215 Spadina Ave, Suite 406, Toronto ON M5T 2C7, Canada
Telephone 1 800 380 4777/1 905 487 7372
E-mail infocanada@crossculturalsolutions.org

UK:
Tower Point 44, North Road, Brighton BN1 1YR
Telephone +44 (0)845 458 2781, 2782 or +44 (0)1273 666392
E-mail infouk@crossculturalsolutions.org

Australia:
PO Box 581, Sydney Markets, NSW 2129, Australia
Telephone +61 (0)2 4368 4176
E-mail infoaustralia@crossculturalsolutions.org
www.crossculturalsolutions.org

Global Vision International (GVI)

Global Vision International provides support and services to international charities, NGOs and governmental agencies. Through its links with over 150 project partners in over 30 countries, it offers volunteering opportunities in environmental research, conservation, education and community development.

3 High Street, St Albans, Hertfordshire AL3 4ED
Telephone +44 (0)1727 250 250
E-mail info@gvi.co.uk
www.gvi.co.uk

Oxfam International

Oxfam International is a confederation of organisations working together in over 100 countries to find lasting solutions to poverty and injustice. It seeks increased worldwide public understanding that economic and social justice is crucial to sustainable development. It also strives to be a global campaigning force promoting the awareness and motivation that comes with global citizenship while seeking to shift public opinion in order to give equity the same priority as economic growth.

Suite 20, 266 Banbury Road, Oxford OX2 7DL
Telephone +44 (0)870 333 2700
(These are the contact details for the UK office;
see website for other Oxfam offices worldwide)
www.oxfam.org

Overseas-based

Aasaman Nepal

Aasaman Nepal aims to get children out of work and into school. Its broader mission is to help develop a society where children have the right to education, survival, development and participation.

http://e-archive.criced.tsukuba.ac.jp/data/doc/ppt/2004/07/Aasaman%20Nepal%20presentation.712.ppt

Albemarle Housing Improvement Program (AHIP)

AHIP is a non-profit housing and community development organisation based in Albemarle County and Charlottesville City. It helps low-income people to obtain secure, safe, decent and affordable housing.

2127 Berkmar Drive, Charlottesville, VA 22901
Telephone (434) 817-AHIP (2447)
E-mail ahip@ahipva.org
www.ahipva.org

Alpamys

Alpamys is an organisation that includes parents of children with disabilities and different specialists and volunteers.

236 Shakhvarostova Street, Taldykorgan, Kazakhstan
Telephone (434) 817-AHIP (2447)
E-mail ahip@ahipva.org
http://alpamys.netfirms.com/ABOUTUS.HTM

Bakti

Bakti is a Malaysian organisation that uses the combined efforts of the wives of its country's leaders to provide assistance to individuals who need help and support. It has many community projects and welfare services relating to education, human development, sports and cultural activities.

Casa da Mulher do Nordeste (The House of Women of the Northeast)

Casa da Mulher do Nordeste is based in Recife, north-east Brazil. It campaigns to improve conditions for female workers and strives to improve their knowledge of their rights.

Rua Alberto Paiva, n. 162, Bairro das Graças, Recife–PE
Telephone (81) 3426 0212 3426 0922
E-mail cmnordeste@uol.com.br
www.tdh.org.br/projetos/cmn/rmpn.shtml

Community–University Partnerships (CUPS)

The office of Community–University Partnerships (CUPS) at the University of the Witwatersrand in Johannesburg bridges academia with society. Its purpose is to enable and promote civic engagement as an active form of academic citizenship. The responsibility of CUPS is to encourage the university to be more responsible to the social and economic needs of society by: developing academically based community service courses in partnership with communities and service providers; fostering extra-curricular activities, which enable civic leadership, community development and institutional change; stimulating collaborative research activities, which address developmental needs in society; and working with institutional processes that enhance civic engagement.

Private Bag X3, Wits, Johannesburg 2050, South Africa
Telephone +27 11 7179732
E-mail assist@partners.wits.ac.za
www.wits.ac.za/AboutWits/Entities/CUPS/CUPSHome.htm

Gerakan Pramuka

Gerakan Pramuka is the national scouting organisation of Indonesia. Its activities have an educational basis and are directed towards the development of a peaceful and prosperous Indonesian community.

Jl. Medan Merdeka Timur 6, Jakarta 10110, Indonesia
Telephone (021) 3507645
E-mail kwarnas@pramuka.or.id/kwarnas@centrin.net.id
www.pramuka.or.id

Hands On Manila (HOM)

Hands On Manila is based in Manila, the capital city of the Philippines. It provides diverse and flexible volunteer opportunities that address the needs of its community.

Unit 10 Lower Penthouse Medical Plaza Building, Amorsolo cor. Dela Rosa Sts, Legaspi Village, Makati City, 1229 Manila, Philippines
Telephone (632) 843 5231
Fax (632) 843 7044
E-mail info@handsonmanila.org
www.handsonmanila.org

Hands On Network

The Hands On Network is based in America. It seeks to transform people and communities and inspire, equip and mobilise people to take action that changes the world. It aims to ensure that there are volunteer and community participation opportunities for people throughout America and increasingly, around the world. It engages individuals, corporations, non-profit organisations and government institutions in developing and mobilising collaborative citizen leadership in pursuit of innovative, actionable solutions that can be replicated across the world.

600 Means Street, Suite 210, Atlanta, GA 30318
Telephone 404 979 2900
E-mail info@handsonnetwork.org
www.handsonnetwork.org

The International Federation of Red Cross and Red Crescent Societies

The International Federation of Red Cross and Red Crescent Societies is the world's largest humanitarian organisation. The International Federation aims to improve the lives of vulnerable people by mobilising the power of humanity. Its programmes are grouped into four main core areas: promoting humanitarian principles and values; disaster response; disaster preparedness; and health and care in the community. Through voluntary action, it seeks a world of empowered communities, better able to address human suffering and crises with hope, respect for dignity and a concern for equity.

PO Box 372, CH-1211 Geneva 19, Switzerland
Telephone +41 22 730 42 22
E-mail via website
www.ifrc.org

Kapamagogopa Inc.

Kapamagogopa is a Muslim volunteering organisation based in Iligan City in the Philippines. It was founded to positively change, through volunteering, the chronic conflict between clans, religion-based differences between Christians and Muslims, and the alienation of indigenous people. It also provides young Muslim adults with professional development opportunities.

Door F6, A and B Apt, Purok Anthurium, Mahayahay 9200, Illigan City, Philippines
Telephone +63 221 5523
E-mail mariambarandia@ki-volunteer.org
www.ki-volunteer.org

Life Vanguards (LIVA)

LIVA is based in Nigeria and focuses on youth health and development. It aims to enhance life options for young people by the provision of information, education, support and other services that will encourage their entrepreneurial skills development, equip them for leadership responsibilities, protect them from sexual and reproductive health problems and groom them to become responsible adults. In general, LIVA's strategic approach and programmes seek to contribute to the holistic development of the youth. It also has a thematic focus on HIV and Aids prevention, care and support and the rehabilitation and resettling of the physically challenged. It offers global and local volunteering programmes and activities.

Life Vanguards House, opposite Jerry Paul Filling Station, Ring Road, PO Box 2182, Osogbo, Osun State, Nigeria
Telephone 035 242738, 243552
E-mail via website
www.lifevanguards.org

Muhammadiyah

Muhammadiyah is an Islamic reformist and socio-religious organisation based in Indonesia. It focuses on social, religious and educational activities, and manages mosques, schools, universities, libraries, hospitals, medical clinics, orphanages and houses for the poor. It also works with various partner organisations in developing international community exchange programmes.

www.muhammadiyah.or.id

Muslim Education and Welfare Association (MEWA)

MEWA is an NGO based in Mombasa, Kenya, which promotes the educational, economic, social and cultural welfare of all Muslims. It is also involved in international community exchange projects, and offers various programmes aimed at improving the educational and welfare status of communities.

PO Box 89427 – 80100, Mombasa, Kenya
Telephone 020 2026134, 041 2493157, 2490272, 0722 819795
E-mail secretariat@mewa.or.ke
www.mewa.or.ke

Nagorik Uddyog (Citizen's Initiative)

Nagorik Uddyog promotes the rights, justice and representation of Bangladeshi women at the grass-roots level. Women are educated about their human rights and rights within the Shalish process, which is the informal judiciary system that deals with local level issues.

E-mail nu@bdmail.net

Pattan

The Pattan Development Organisation is based in Pakistan and works with the powerless and most vulnerable people in the Riverine communities of the Punjab province. Its primary mandate is to help the communities on the issues of disaster preparedness, management and mitigation. It focuses on harnessing the unreleased social and political potential of people in an effort to enable them to take control of the decisions that affect their daily lives. It seeks to facilitate the creation of local level institutions that could represent and articulate the interests of all social groups, breaking the barriers by traditional power structures.

National office:
House No. 5, Street 58, F-10/3, Islamabad, Pakistan
Telephone +92 51 2299494, 2211875
Fax +92 51 2291547
www.pattan.org

National field office (Pakistan Disaster Preparedness and Learning Centre):
Mauza Bahadurpur, Bosan Road, Multan, Pakistan, PO Box 607, GPO Multan, Pakistan
Telephone +92 61 223572
Fax +92 61 220801

Pravah

Pravah is based in New Delhi, India. It works with adolescents, youth organisations and institutions working with young people to have an impact on social justice by means of a broad spectrum of programmes that aim to inspire, streamline and facilitate youth citizenship action.

C-24 B, Second Floor, Kalkaji, New Delhi 110019, India
Telephone +91 11 2644 0619, 2621 3918, 2644 0619
E-mail mail@pravah.org
www.pravah.org
www.younginfluencers.com

Samigos

Samigos is a non-profit organisation based in South Africa and Mozambique. It strives for a strong regional community where all the people of South Africa, Mozambique and SADC as a whole, can benefit from fruitful and peaceful economic, social and cultural interaction and development. It aims to strengthen ties of friendship and understanding by improving mutual understanding through people-to-people dialogue and action. It also seeks to contribute to the development of organisational and leadership skills with a strategic focus on educational and community activities.

www.samigos.org
(Samigos can be contacted via their website)

SOS Corpo

SOS Corpo is a community organisation in north-east Brazil that campaigns for gender inequality through strategies of knowledge, education and political action.

Contact by webmail webmail.soscorpo.org.br
www.soscorpo.org.br

Voluntary Workcamps Association of Ghana (VOLU)

VOLU is based in Accra, Ghana. It builds schools and community centres, plants trees in deforested areas, and organises HIV and Aids education campaigns as well as other activities. It offers three- to four-week voluntary workcamps with both Ghanaian and international volunteers.

PO Box 1540, Accra, Ghana
Telephone +233 21 663486
E-mail info@voluntaryworkcamps.org
www.voluntaryworkcamps.org/www.volunteerafrica.org/blue/volu.html

VSO Bahaginan

VSO Bahaginan is a development organisation committed to fighting global poverty and disadvantage through a wide range of volunteer development programmes. As a member of VSO Federation, it recruits, trains and matches volunteers from the Philippines to placements that meet the requests of its overseas partners.

Unit 505 Pacific Corporate Center, 131 West Avenue, Quezon City, Philippines
Telephone (632) 3746450–52
E-mail bahaginan@vsoint.org
www.vsobahaginan.org.ph

Wits Volunteer Programme (WVP)

In the University of the Witwatersrand in Johannesburg, the Wits Volunteer Programme pursues a university community that engages closely with civil society in a socially responsive manner to contribute towards the development of a society for the well-being of the population as a whole. It fosters extra-curricular activities that enable civic leadership, community development and institutional change.

Private Bag X3, Wits, Johannesburg, 2050, South Africa
Telephone +27 11 7179732
E-mail assist@partners.wits.ac.za
web.wits.ac.za/AboutWits/Entities/CUPS/WVP/volunteering.htm

Young Power in Social Action (YPSA)

YPSA is a development organisation in Bangladesh that seeks to eradicate poverty and secure the basic needs and rights of all people. It works with poor and vulnerable people to help them produce their own and their community's sustainable development.

House # F10 (P), Road # 13, Block-B, Chandgaon R/A, Chittagong 4212, Bangladesh
Telephone +88 031 672857
E-mail info@ypsa.org
www.ypsa.org

Youth Association for Population and Development (YAPD)

YAPD is based in Cairo and encourages youth to participate in the development of their local community through voluntary work. It has accumulated a broad range of experience and innovations in many fields, including research, advocacy, training, facilitation and technical assistance. As well as volunteering and training, its activities concern women and children, health, information and international communication, environment, education, and rural–urban immigration.

www.yapd.org.eg

Useful websites

www.oneworld.net/action/volunteers

www.volunteerafrica.org

www.oneworld.net

www.yearoutgroup.org

www.greenvol.com

www.jobsincharity.co.uk

www.do-it.org.uk

www.support4learning.org.uk

www.idealist.org